Letter from the Editors

We returned from our yearly research trip in March, and the fruits of that labor will begin to appear in this issue of the magazine. We also have features planned for the rest of the year that we think you're going to love.

The format of the magazine allows us to focus on topics and places that wouldn't necessarily work on our website, but work great in print because we can share more pictures and dedicate more words. It's very freeing to finally have a venue to write about the things we love about England the most.

The big feature in this issue is our exploration of the history of British Airways - a topic I'm very passionate about. I'm also really chuffed to share the photos from our tour of Churchill's Secret Bunker at Down Street. We've also got great new columns from Laurence and Erin on top of everything else you can expect in each issue - poems, songs, art, and more.

Springtime is a very special time in England - the bluebells bloom and Britain's beautiful gardens come into flower. The weather begins to warm and the days start to get longer on their march towards summer. Oh, how I wish I could pop over to my 'local' stately home and have a wander around the rooms and gardens, hear the British birdsong, and smell the lovely flowers.

Happy Reading!

Cheers,
Jonathan & Jackie
Anglotopia

Table of Contents

A Very British Airline......................................2
Brit Book Corner..10
Poem...12
Then & Now..14
Song..16
Top 10 Winchester...18
Great British Icons - The Police Box...........22
Lost in the Pond...24
William III..26
Milton Abbas..30
Great British Art..34
This English Life...36
Great British Questions................................39
The Great Smog of 1952................................40
London Bookshop Dreams...........................44
Great Britons: William Morris.....................50
Churchill's Secret Bunker.............................54
The Slang Page..60

About the Magazine

The Anglotopia Magazine is published quarterly by Anglotopia LLC, a USA registered Corporation. All contents copyrighted and may not be reproduced without permission.

Letters to the Editors may be addressed to:

Anglotopia LLC
1101 Cumberland Crossing #120
Valparaiso, IN 46383
USA

Photos: Cover: Cottage in Milton Abbas. Back cover: Winchester Cathedral. Inside Back Cover: King Alfred's Tower, Stourhead, Wiltshire

A Very British Airline

British Airways' Past and Present

By Jonathan Thomas

A British Airways Airbus A380 Flies Over the White Cliffs of Dover

Did you know that there is a way to travel to Britain before you even arrive there? Visit any international airport where British Airways flies out of and get on any one of their planes. As soon as you step onto a British Airways aircraft, you've arrived in England. I don't mean technically in legal terms. I mean that by flying British Airways, you fly the most British way possible. The crew is British and will greet you warmly. They will hand you British newspapers. There is classical music playing over the intercom - often a British composer like Elgar or Vaughn-Williams. They'll serve British food. Much of the entertainment on board will be British. Once those doors shut and the plane begins to depart, you've already arrived in England like magic, even though you won't actually be there for a few hours.

British Airways is almost 100 years old and traces its roots back to the very first international passenger flights. Springing from the earlier airline BOAC, and now part of International Airlines Group, the airline has a long history of acquisitions, mergers, nationalisation, and privatisation. It has always been an innovator, running the first commercial jet airplanes, as well as the world's only supersonic passenger flights. Supported by the UK government for its first 68 years, it ran losses for much of that time but continued to grow and develop. Following its sale to the public, it has remained profitable and growing, through the turbulent end of the 20th century that destroyed many other airlines. Its fleet has included almost all of the most iconic aircraft, and it continues to be a prestigious airline, despite ongoing staff disputes and changes to remain profitable in a highly competitive market.

It's a fascinating and wide-ranging history. I have my own personal history with the airline. We're based just outside of Chicago, and we're lucky that British Airways flies two direct routes from O'Hare to London every day. Every trip I've been on to England from 2001 until now has been on British Airways (14 trips in total!). I would not fly any other way and would feel like I'm betraying BA if I did. Of course, like any airline, things don't always go smoothly (I've experienced my share of unexpected delays and broken bathrooms in flight). But through it all British Airways always provides a top-notch experience, and it has been very supportive of *Anglotopia* in its 10-year history. Last year, BA invited us to visit their museum near Heathrow Airport and this year we accepted an invitation to test out their latest product offerings. But first, let's look at the history of British Airways and how it has evolved over the years.

On an August day in 1919, the first World War finally ended, a single-engine De Havilland biplane took off from Hounslow Heath, an open, treeless area close to the site where Heathrow Airport sits today. Besides the pilot, it carried a single passenger and his luggage. The plane also carried a small cargo of newspapers, jam, clotted cream, and several brace of grouse. A short time later it landed in Paris. It was the world's first international commercial flight, and a new mode of mass transport had been born. A week later a second one-plane airline, Handley Page Transport Ltd, began flying the same route, using converted twin-engine WWI bombers.

Through multiple mergers and restructuring, Handley Page, with a cluster of other early British commercial airlines, would become British Airways. Indeed, the pilot of that first Handley Page flight would become a chairman in the BA network. Today that airline operates 268 aircraft flying to 183 global destinations, with annual revenues of more than £11 billion. It has the largest fleet of any British airline and is second only to the upstart EasyJet in the number of passengers carried. It is the sixth-largest airline globally by revenue.

From the beginning, the British government saw a need to step in and control the development of the new industry. A parliamentary Standing Advisory Committee on Civil Aviation recommended that "The proper place for initial action" in joining the parts of the British Empire together by this new means of transport was a route to India and from

Key Facts

- Descended from the very first British commercial airlines
- Ran both the first jet and the first supersonic passenger flights
- Originally supported by government subsidies and ownership
- Today the UK's largest airline by fleet size, with 268 planes flying to 183 destinations.

Imperial Airways' The Dorado, an Imperial Airways-operated De Havilland DH86

there on to Australia. It saw the development of a service to South Africa shortly after that, with Canada and New Zealand not far behind. Most importantly, it decided that the best way to develop these Imperial routes was by using a hybrid model of private enterprise backed by State support.

In 1924, the government organised a merger among most of the small carriers then operating, creating Imperial Airways. This new company began operating to several European capitals from a new airfield at Croydon, with test flights to Africa, India, and the Middle East. At the end of 1930, a new, luxurious aircraft was inaugurated, the Handley Page H.P.42. It carried 24 passengers – already segregated into two classes – on longer hauls to India, and 28 to Europe, since less luggage space was needed for the shorter hauls.

As the demand for service grew rapidly, Imperial Airways took either a huge gamble or a visionary move, depending on your viewpoint, by ordering 28 long-range monoplane flying boats of an undeveloped design from Short Brothers, a company based in Belfast that is still operating today. The plane became known as the Short Empire. Flying boats were seen as the future of aviation at the time, and the Short Empire could carry 17 passengers and a large payload of cargo and mail, flying 700 miles before refueling. This allowed it to go to South Africa and Australia in short hops, but the Atlantic was more challenging. Only in 1939 would the airline begin regular transatlantic flights to Montreal and New York, using flying boats which refueled in flight.

Smaller airlines continued to exist, and in 1935 most of these merged to form British Airways Limited. In 1939, following the outbreak of WWII, the government merged that airline with Imperial to form the British Overseas Airways Corporation (BOAC). Civil aviation had been suspended with the war, and BOAC was put on a war footing. Routes were diverted from crossing Europe to flying through Cairo, and a variety of new planes were put into service to cope with the needs of wartime passenger flights. With their limited fuel capacity, the flying boats began to fade from service, and airports on land were beginning to spread and develop. BOAC did continue to use them until 1950, long after other airlines had ceased operating them.

At the end of the war, BOAC was looking at a fleet of very diverse aircraft, and facilities scattered around the globe. It would take a decade to centralise their operations at Heathrow and to create a more standardised fleet. When they began looking for new aircraft, a dispute soon developed that would mark the company's relationship with its unions and the governments for decades. Should they buy American planes or support British manufacturers? With uncertain local suppliers, and in the face of significant opposition, they persuaded a bankrupt government to release precious American dollars to buy six Lockheed Constellations and six Boeing Stratocruisers, the most advanced passenger planes at the time, with pressurised cabins. They continued to build a fleet of these planes by acquiring them from other airlines. They did 'Buy British' in the shape of the Handley Page Hermes, but also added Douglas DC-7Cs.

By the mid-1950s the fleet began to resemble aircraft we would travel in today, but they were, of course, all propeller-driven planes. In 1952, the BOAC took the lead, with the world's first commercial jetliner, the British de Havilland DH 106 Comet. These early jets were grounded within two years after four crashes, two by BOAC planes. Design modifications overcame the weaknesses in the fuselage, and new, safer Comets were soon back in the air. Throughout this period the company steadily lost money, and consistently recorded losses. Despite a brief period of profitability in 1963–1966, its debt stood at approximately £80 million by 1964, all borrowed from the government. A large part of this loss came from the insistent of the Government that the company purchase only British planes. The company had been lent £180 million to buy 35 Vickers VC10 jets it did not want, and believed would keep it unprofitable. A new chairman, Sir Giles Guthrie, came onboard in 1964 with a mandate to make the company profitable, and the Vickers' purchase was reduced to 17 planes. The iconic Boeing 707 was added to the list – although two of those also crashed – and the company was significantly restructured. With increased traffic, the larger Boeing 747 entered service in 1970, but it was to take a year for flights to begin due to protracted disputes with the unions over pay rates for manning the new plane.

In 1972, BOAC and its sister company British European Airways (BEA) merged to form a new company, British Airways. Innovating again, it began a supersonic trans-Atlantic route between

An old Imperial Airways travel poster and route map

London and New York with the Concorde, a joint Anglo-French project. Dubbed a 'white elephant' by the media, projected supersonic routes to India and Australia never became a reality. Concorde made its last flight in 2003.

Serious changes appeared on the horizon for BA with the arrival of Margaret Thatcher at 10 Downing Street. With a new economic outlook shared by her friend, American President Ronald Reagan, she began an aggressive campaign to sell the many industries which at that time were owned by the government. The only problem was that no one would buy the company as a loss-making business, so drastic steps had to be taken. By 1991, Thatcher was gone, but the policy of selling government-owned businesses continued, and a new Chairman of the Board, Sir John King, and then a new CEO, Colin Marshall, set about making the company profitable. They promoted Concorde to develop a prestigious image for the company and shed 23,000 employees. By making very generous

The Concorde was long considered BA's flagship aircraft but it was retired in 2003

redundancy payments, they managed to do that while simultaneously boosting the morale of the remaining employees. The price-tag of those generous pay-outs – almost half a billion pounds – was picked up by the government, but the company now had an attractive, profitable image to attract buyers.

After further route consolidations, the company went public with a share offering in 1987. The initial purchase was nine times oversubscribed. The company has remained largely profitable since then, although there have been several turbulent periods with the changes in airlines, and world economic downturns. BA grew dramatically following privatisation, as international air travel grew globally. Profits grew three-fold, passenger miles increased, while employee numbers remained constant, and have fallen slightly in recent years. Numerous acquisitions of smaller airlines took place, new routes and new lower-cost subsidiaries were established as the market continued to evolve.

During the 1980s, the airline aggressively took on a new rival, Virgin Atlantic Airways, founded by Richard Branson. Determined to stop this upstart in its tracks, they began a disinformation campaign that ended with Branson suing BA for libel in 1992. Seeing defeat in the courts looming, BA settled, and Branson scored publicity points by dividing the settlement (a total of £610,00)among his staff as a so-called 'BA bonus.' Bitterness and rivalry between the airlines would continue for years. In 1992 BA purchased 44 percent of USAir Inc. and then sold it again in 1997. In 1998 it joined the Oneworld global alliance with other international airlines, with the goal of capturing the lucrative frequent flyer market.

BA entered the modern era by merging with the Spanish airline Iberia in 2011. BA became the majority shareholder in the new company, called International Consolidated Airlines Group, S.A, or IAG. The various airlines in the group, including the Irish Aer Lingus and the Spanish low-cost airline Vueling, plus several BA subsidiaries such as OpenSkies and the Scandinavian SUN-AIR, operate under their own names. Qatar Air is a major shareholder, with a 20% stake in IAG. As an indication of the diversity of BA operations, visitors to London may be surprised to learn that the popular London Eye observation wheel on the bank of the Thames was developed and originally owned by BA (it's now sponsored by another company).

Most recently, they've sponsored the British Airways i360 Observation Tower that just opened in Brighton.

The shining beacon of British Airways right now is Terminal Five; its hub is at Heathrow Airport. It's rare for an airline to have it's own dedicated terminal but BA has it at Heathrow because of the scale of their operations. One plane takes off every 45 seconds at Heathrow, and almost half of those are BA or IAG aircraft. T5 was, for many years, Britain's biggest construction project. It cost £4 billion and took 20 years from conception to completion. It is the largest free-standing structure in the UK. When is opened in 2008, there were teething problems, but they have all been worked out now.

When I mention to some people that I love flying into Terminal Five, they laugh a bit. But the building is simply beautiful. It's a glowing glass box, designed perfectly for air travel. It's clean. It's airy. It's a much better passenger experience than when you used to arrive in the old and now demolished terminals at Heathrow. It's a proper welcome to Britain.

During our most recent trip, we were invited to the arrivals lounge in Terminal Five. It's a relaxing and hospitable space where you can take a shower after your flight, get a hot breakfast, and plan your day ahead in London. If you're a business traveler, it's a great way to hit the ground running in London. We ate breakfast, caught up with the news and the emails waiting for us and when we were ready, headed to get our hire car. It was such a breath of fresh air to stop and recharge before getting to work. Of course, you have to be invited into the arrivals lounge (by virtue of buying a Business or First class ticket), so it's quite a treat.

Our journey this past February began with our arrival at Chicago's O'Hare Airport. We were scheduled on the late afternoon flight to London. We were warmly welcomed by BA staff as we checked our bags and we sailed through security. As most international flights depart in the evening at O'Hare, we beat the rush and didn't have to deal with a long security queue. We immediately made our way to the British Airways lounge where staff we expecting us. They welcomed us warmly, we've traveled so much in the last few years, they've started to recognise the folks from Anglotopia, and it's a special treat to be known.

This time around, though, we had a special

Your correspondents in the 'King & Queen' seats

treat that we never had before. We were welcomed by invitation into the First Class Lounge. I should say that the BA lounge for Club World travelers is fantastic. So, we were in for a treat to be invited to the First Lounge. It's a small dining room, private from the rest of the lounge. You have your own waiter and separate menu from what's served to everyone else in the lounge along with a fantastic wine selection. It was surprising that we were the only ones in there - we had the whole First Class lounge to ourselves! We enjoyed a fantastic pre-flight meal - one of the best we've ever had. The time also passed quickly.

When we finished with dinner, we crossed over the airside First Class lounge to wait for boarding and just when we'd sat down; it was time to board our flight. The First Lounge has its own entrance to the plane, so you don't have to wait in line for boarding. Our plane that day was a Boeing 777-200ER, a massive plane that was relatively new. All the interiors felt new and fresh. I've been on some old planes, so I know what it's like.

We had seats in Club World for this trip, which is why it was such a treat to be able to use the First Lounge. Club World, or Business Class, is the way we love to travel if we have the opportunity. BA Club World has one important, key feature. The seats go almost completely flat. This means that you can sleep like you're in a bed on an overnight flight to London. This allows you to arrive in London completely rested and ready to make the most of your first day in England. I'm incapable of sleeping in a regular economy seat - I cannot sleep sitting up. So, I usually arrive in London not well rested and become a zombie for the first day. It feels like such a

Top: New look Club World seats on the revamped 747's. Bottom: A look at Club World on the 747 Upper Deck

waste to lose almost an entire day in London when they're so precious. So, if we have the opportunity to fly Club World, I can sleep on the plane and make the most of my trip.

In addition to the seat lying flat, we were in the middle aisle of the plane, so we had the 'King and Queen' seats, it's like being in your own little private cabin. You have large screens to watch BA's great selection of in-flight entertainment. All the seats have USB charging ports so we could have our phones fully charged for our arrival. After takeoff, Mrs. Anglotopia went right to sleep. I opted to eat again during the in-flight service and watched a movie while I ate a delicious stuffed chicken meal. The food in Club World is always fantastic, way better than what you usually get in economy. After eating and enjoying a movie, I made the seat flat and went to sleep. I hope up about an hour before landing refreshed and ready to explore England.

We arrived early to Terminal Five - the sun was not even up yet! We even got a parking space right at the main T5 building (most later flights end up at one of the satellite terminals). When I mention to some people that I love flying into Terminal Five, they snigger a bit. But the building is simply beautiful. It's a glowing glass box, designed perfectly for air travel. It's clean. It's airy. It's a much better passenger experience than when you used to arrive in the old and now demolished terminals at Heathrow. It's a proper welcome to Britain. During our most recent trip, we were invited to the arrivals lounge in Terminal Five. It's a relaxing and hospitable space where you can take a shower after your flight, get a hot breakfast and plan your day ahead in London. If you're a business traveler, it's a great way to hit the ground running in London. We ate breakfast, caught up with the news and the emails waiting for us and when we were ready, headed to get our hire car. It was such a breath of fresh air to stop and recharge before getting to work. Of course, you have to be invited into the arrivals lounge (by virtue of buying a Business or First class ticket), so it's quite a treat.

Our flight home from London was just over a week later after a whirlwind trip exploring London and Dorset. Our flight was early this time, we were leaving at noon (we usually take the late afternoon flight home) so we got to the airport early. We checked in at the special check-in area for Business Class and sailed through security. We had an invitation to the Galleries lounge at Terminal Five, another special treat for us. We love the lounges at Terminal Five. The Terminal is huge and bustling, so the Galleries lounges are quiet respites away from the noise. They have a lovely terrace where you can sit and watch beautiful planes take off and land on both runways at Heathrow. They serve breakfast and lunch. There are ample free newspapers and magazines.

As a bit of an airplane nut, I look forward to flying every time. But that day I was in for a special treat. We were due to fly home on a Boeing 747, which itself isn't that special. This time, though, our Club World seats were on the upper deck of the 747. I'd never been up there. On BA's fleet, the Upper Deck is exclusively Club World. You're completely separate from the rest of the plane. Flying in BA's Club World Upper Deck was like flying in your own private jet. There was plenty of room - a bit more than there usually is in Club World. The staff are helpful (I had some airsickness on the way home and the staff were very concerned and helpful). We felt like we were flying in style on our private jet. It's also much smoother on the upper deck if we had turbulence going home, I didn't feel it, and you barely hear the roar of the 747s four engines. As an AV geek, I was in heaven. We were served a delicious meal; it's always a treat to eat a steak at 30,000 feet!

BA's fleet of 747s was recently refurbished so all the interiors were new and we loved the new LED mood lighting. It felt like a brand new plane. It was a treat to fly in one because 747s are on their way out in the fleets of global airlines. They're fuel hungry and inefficient compared to the newer 777s and 787s. BA still flies about forty 747s, and all of them have been refurbished. They plan to keep flying them for several years to come - well into the 2020s but it was nice to get a chance to fly in the upper deck of a 747 before I lose the opportunity to do so.

The airline continues to innovate. British Airways recently announced a massive investment into the airline. They plan to upgrade their lounges all over the world, including at New York's JFK Airport. They will spend £65m alone at JFK where they have 20 flights a day to London serving more than 100,000 passengers a year. They also plan to spend £500m in refurbishing Club World across their entire fleet as well as adding WiFi to their long haul flights.

Heritage. That's what sets BA apart from all the other major airlines. They have almost 100 years of history. And they're proud of it. They wear it on their sleeves. Their motto is: To Fly, To Serve. They do both things brilliantly. The international airline game is continually changing, British Airways has changed with it, but one thing hasn't changed: their respect for their own heritage and their desire to be the best airline in the world as a beacon of Britishness all over the world. I can't wait for my next flight.

Further Reading

- British Airways: An Illustrated History by Paul Jarvis
- British Airways: Engineering an Airline15 by Paul Jarvis
- History of British European Airways: 1946 - 1972 by Charles Woodley
- Airline: The Inside Story of British Airways By Arthur Reed
- Concorde by Christopher Orlebar

Sites to Visit

British Airways maintains a Heritage Collection of historic artifacts at its museum at its Waterside headquarters not far from Heathrow Airport. The museum is run by volunteers from ex-BA staff, and is only open for limited hours, by appointment. We were given a personal tour on a previous trip, and it was a real treat. They an extensive collection of memorabilia, including Imperial Airways Posters, and many models of old and new BA planes. As well there are timetables, uniforms, menus and even washbags from different eras. There's also a small gift shop where you can buy BA posters, books and more (the author of the books I bought happened to be there and signed them!). The museum is not open to the public, but you can request a tour. An appointment can be requested at http://www.bamuseum.com.

All of BA's former Concordes are now on display in museums around the world. You can see them at Manchester Airport, National Museum of Flight in Edinburgh, Intrepid Air & Sea Museum in New York City, Barbados, Museum of Flight in Seattle and Aerospace Bristol Museum opening in 2017. One BA Concorde is still in BA's possession and sits at Heathrow, you can occasionally see it when taxiing for take-off or after you've landed - it's not on public display.

BRIT BOOK CORNER

London Uncovered by Peter Dazeley and Mark Daly

I was a huge fan of photographer Peter Dazeley's last book, Unseen London, which showcased many places in London that are often closed off from the public. The book was so popular that Peter wanted to do another book, this time with a focus on places that people could actually visit - but with the proviso they are unique in some way. London Uncovered is an interesting tour around lesser-known London places but also places you already may be familiar with. They're brought to life by Peter's superb photography that is unmatched by anyone else shooting in London today. The added text by Mark Daly adds to the book as the context and history of each place is explained. They also helpfully tell you how to visit each place. It's a bit large to be a guidebook, but it's a great book to have as a reference so when you're planning your next trip to London, you can plan to visit some places you might not normally think of. My favorite places featured in the book are the hotel at St Pancras International Railway Station, Apsley House, Churchill War Rooms and Charterhouse (a former monastery that happens to be London's newest museum). The books weighs in at more than 300 beautiful full-color pages, and it's divided into eight sections: Historical Homes, Food & Drink, Palaces of Entertainment, Places of Worship Remarkable Shops, Science, and Education, The Inns of Court and Unusual Museums. This book is a treasure, and I will gladly add it to my library. Peter all have another book out later this year about London theatres, and we can't wait to see his latest pictures! Francis Lincoln $50

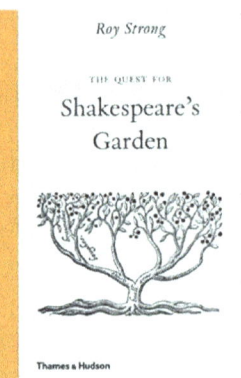

The Quest for Shakespeare's Garden by Roy Strong

This new book put together by Sir Roy Strong, a prominent British art historian and critic, is a look at Shakespeare and his relationship with gardens and nature. This lavishly illustrated history of gardens draws from Shakespeare's works and garden writing. Published in association with the Shakespeare Birthplace Trust, The Quest for Shakespeare's Garden traces the origins of garden history and the Elizabethan garden, as well as telling the story of the Bard's own garden in Stratford-upon-Avon. Roy Strong's detailed account is inspired by Shakespeare's works and supplemented by Francis Bacon's 1625 essay "Of Gardens" which provides Elizabethan-era advice to garden enthusiasts on such topics as topiary, seasonal gardens, scents, aviaries, and more. It's a beautifully put together book and a must for any fan of Shakespeare. Thames & Hudson $19.95

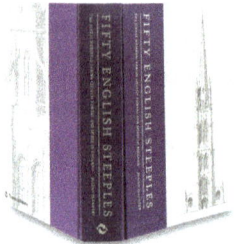

50 English Steeples by Julian Flannery

A close look at the quintessential English steeple by way of the fifty most significant of the past five hundred years, complemented by gorgeous photographs and immaculate illustrations. The picturesque English town would be nothing without its steeple - you can spot them quite easily as they're usually the tallest structure in a town. Fifty English Steeples tours the fifty most important medieval parish church towers and spires in England, covering a period of some 500 years. With much history covered, this elegant volume represents five years of painstaking original research, captured in the informative text, high-quality new photography, and 175 immaculately presented line drawings. The introduction provides an overview of the technological and aesthetic development of steeples and their medieval origins which would make a fascinating book in itself. The chapters that follow are devoted to a richly illustrated survey of the most beautiful and historically significant towers and spires in England, from renowned Saxon churches such as Earls Barton to those of almost cathedral proportions such as Salle in Norfolk or Chipping Campden in the heart of the Cotswolds. Flannery's outstanding technical drawings of all fifty steeples complement this beautifully illustrated tome and help to shed new light on each tower and spire as a testament to achievements of England in the Middle Ages. Frances Lincoln SRP $85.00

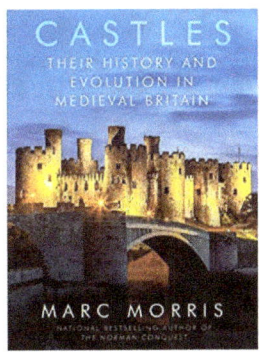

Castles by Marc Morris

This quick read by Marc Morris is an excellent overview of the history of castles during England's Medieval period. When William the Conqueror invaded in 1066, castles were largely unknown to England - they were a new French invention (and the Anglo-Saxons weren't too fond of anything French). But William remade Britain by bringing the French idea of castles over to England, building more than 500 of them in fact. This fascinating book explores this quickly and then ends with a lovely explanation of why castles fell out of fashion (and eventually replaced by Stately Homes). If you are fascinated by castles, you will enjoy this book. Pegasus Books $27.95

Places of the Mind: British Watercolor Landscapes 1850-1950

Released to coincide with a new exhibition as the British Museum (running from February 2017 to August 2017), Places of the Mind seeks to show the development of watercolor art and how artists tried to not only create beautiful landscapes, but also create a certain feeling that the landscapes evoke. Some do this more successfully than others. The book is filled with 159 beautiful color illustrations and it features some of the finest watercolors ever painted in British art history. My personal favorite was Cowdray Cottage by Helen Allingham, such a beautiful and idyllic country scene (which is itself misleading as the book notes - rural life was miserable for most people). This paperback book provides a fascinating and fresh perspective on Victorian and Modern era watercolor painting. Thames & Hudson $29.95

New Architecture London by Richard Schulman and Agnese Sanvito

London is a two thousand-year-old city, and there are elements of its age all over the city. London's architecture has changed over the centuries, and its look and feel has never been homogenous. Every new style has faced criticism as it was built next to the old. The buildings built in the last 30-40 years are no different. Many people are offended by the site of modern architecture in London, but many people also welcome it. This new book celebrates the most beautiful of the new buildings - from The Shard, The Gherkin, One New Change and much more. Many of the new buildings have become iconic parts of the London Skyline. Some others really don't fit in with their surroundings. One thing is certain, these buildings will endure for hundreds of years and will become beloved as London grows and grows. This new book by Prestel is a great tribute to these buildings, filled with beautiful photographs. Each building has a quick paragraph on the background of each building (who designed it, their inspirations, etc.). It's a light read and a great introduction to London's newest buildings. Prestel $45

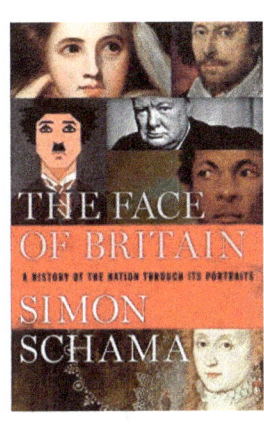

The Face of Britain by Simon Schama

When I hear the name Simon Schama, I immediately take notice. The brilliant author of "A History of Britain" has come out with a new British history book, this time looking at history from the perspective of Art and how British artists portrayed leaders and important historical figures. Based on his recent BBC series of the same name, this book is a fascinating look at British Art History. I was particularly enthralled by the chapter on Sir Winston Churchill and the Sutherland Portrait Controversy (which was dramatized brilliantly recently in Netflix's The Crown). Schama tells the story brilliantly and engagingly and does so throughout the entire book. Many of Britain's most famous Royal and Political portraits are covered here, and it provides an interesting look at the artists and the relationships with their subjects (and also the great historical forces of the time). Oxford University Press $39.95

Spring, the sweet spring

Thomas Nashe - 1600

Spring, the sweet spring, is the year's pleasant king,
Then blooms each thing, then maids dance in a ring,
Cold doth not sting, the pretty birds do sing:
    Cuckoo, jug-jug, pu-we, to-witta-woo!

The palm and may make country houses gay,
Lambs frisk and play, the shepherds pipe all day,
And we hear aye birds tune this merry lay:
    Cuckoo, jug-jug, pu-we, to-witta-woo!

The fields breathe sweet, the daisies kiss our feet,
Young lovers meet, old wives a-sunning sit,
In every street these tunes our ears do greet:
    Cuckoo, jug-jug, pu-we, to witta-woo!
    Spring, the sweet spring!

THEN

This aerial photo of St Paul's Cathedral and the City of London was taken in 1921. This photo is part of a collection that was created by Aerofilms Ltd, a pioneering air survey company set up in 1919 by First World War veterans Francis Lewis Wills and Claude Grahame-White. Their goal was to provide a complete aerial survey of Britain. This striking picture of the City of London features no skyscrapers; the tallest building is clearly St Paul's Cathedral in the center. But more striking are the various Wren-built churches dotted throughout the City of London that were built after the Great Fire of London in 1666. The bridge in the foreground is the Cannon St Railway Bridge which leads into Cannon St Railway Station. Another striking feature of the image is that the city is covered in dark grime, which was the result of coal pollution as most homes and businesses used the fuel for heating. At this point in history, the Thames was very much a working river and you can see many barges and boats.

NOW

The same view today is much changed. First, the most remarkable change is that you no longer need to be in an airplane to get the same view, you can get it from The View from the Shard, the viewing platform in Europe's tallest building located in Southwark. St Paul's is still very much one of the tallest buildings in the picture, though the height of many of the surrounding buildings is now higher. This is because the views around St Paul's are legally protected. However, most of the buildings in the 1921 picture have been swept away. The biggest culprit is bombing damage from World War II. The next biggest culprit is real estate redevelopment post-WWII. However, you can still spot the spires of Wren's churches. The massive train shed at Cannon St was demolished, and now it's a more modern and utilitarian building. London is also much cleaner; the grime has been washed away. The Thames no longer has as much trading activity, so the barges and docks are gone as shipping moved to Felixstowe. The Clean Air Acts of the 1950s banned coal heating, and once the buildings got a good scrubbing, London began to shine.

I Vow to Thee, My Country

By Sir Cecil Spring Rice

I vow to thee, my country, all earthly things above,
Entire and whole and perfect, the service of my love;
The love that asks no question, the love that stands the test,
That lays upon the altar the dearest and the best;
The love that never falters, the love that pays the price,
The love that makes undaunted the final sacrifice.

And there's another country, I've heard of long ago,
Most dear to them that love her, most great to them that know;
We may not count her armies, we may not see her King;
Her fortress is a faithful heart, her pride is suffering;
And soul by soul and silently her shining bounds increase,
And her ways are ways of gentleness, and all her paths are peace.

The path down to Durdle Door, Dorset

TOP TEN WINCHESTER
Exploring Alfred the Great's Capital

Our first stop on a recent trip to England was Winchester. I read in multiple places that it was not only considered the finest English city, that it was the best place to visit and also the best place to live. Surely, this place must be wonderful if so many people claim it is. So, when we landed in England and picked up our hire car, we headed straight for Winchester for the day.

Winchester has a long and storied history. It's mostly known now as one of the original capital cities in England - it was the capital of the Kingdom of Wessex when Alfred the Great ruled Wessex. The city retains much of its medieval character, and there is also a major Jane Austen connection as she spent most of her life in Hampshire.

We found it to be a lovely city. Here's are recommendations for the ten things you must do if you happen to visit, which you should.

Self-Guided Walk

Visit Winchester, the official tourist information center located in the Guildhall building should be your first stop when you visit Winchester. They have ample brochures and guides on what to see and do in the city. Be sure to pick up the self-guided tour pamphlet. This features a map of the city centre and guideposts to all the major attractions within the city. It also gives you several different routes to follow. This guide was invaluable. It's free in the TIC, or you can print one off at home. The helpful staff inside will also be able to direct you to anything you want to see. We particularly enjoyed the bit of the walk that took us along the river and hit all the major sites including Jane Austen's death house (see below).

Winchester Cathedral

Winchester's major landmark is Winchester Cathedral, one of the largest cathedrals in Europe, with the distinction of having the longest nave and overall length of all Gothic cathedrals in Europe. We've seen quite a few English cathedrals, and Winchester is quite a treat. You have to pay to get in, but entry is good for one year. There are guided tours which we recommend as the knowledgeable guides will give you a great overview of all the history in the building.

Jane Austen's Death House and Grave

If not for the faded blue plaque on the outside of this rather downmarket looking yellow house, nestled next to Winchester College (the oldest public school in England), you would walk by it and wish the owners would give it a fresh coat of paint. But this house has an important Jane Austen connection. She spent the final weeks of her life and died in the house. The house is a private home, it is not open to the public, but it is there as a sad memorial to her short life. Across the road, there is a lovely small garden dedicated to her. She was buried in Winchester Cathedral, and when you visit it, you should pass by her grave and pay your respects to one of the finest writers in world history. If you want to experience a place, she actually lived for a long period of time that's a museum, then consider visiting Jane Austen's House in nearby Chawton which is open to the public daily.

Winchester Castle/Great Hall - King Arthur Table Hall

Due to its age, Winchester, of course, has a connection to the mythical King Arthur. If Arthurian legends interest you, then stop by The Great Hall which his home to the Round Table. Now, it's not actually King Arthur's round table. In fact, it's a later recreation commissioned by Edward I to celebrate the marriage of his children in 1290. The table is quite a piece of medieval artwork and a treat to see in person. The thing is 18 feet in diameter, weighs more than 1 ton and made of 12 separate pieces of English Oak. While the table is the main attraction, the Great Hall itself is a beautiful space. It's the only surviving structure from the original Winchester Castle (which was later destroyed after the English Civil War) and one of the finest preserved great halls in England. I would argue that it's almost as impressive at the Great Hall in the Palace of Westminster. When we visited, it was late afternoon, and we practically had the place to ourselves so could linger as long as we wanted. Oddly, we encountered a fellow American working in the gift shop which is always a delight.

Lunch in a pub with a view

After you've done the short walk around the city center, you will likely find yourself quite peckish for tea or lunch. There are plenty of places on the High Street to eat (including - horror - fast food). But since you're in England, why not enjoy a pub lunch? Right off the close leading to Winchester Cathedral is a lovely pub called The William Walker that dates back to 1845. The pub is named after a chap who donned a deep sea diving suit to help repair foundation problems under the cathedral (which has water in the crypt). Walker worked underground in water to shore up the foundations of the building for six years. It is estimated that some 25,000 bags of concrete, 115,000 concrete blocks, and 900,000 bricks were used in the operation. The pub is a fitting tribute - it's certainly been well taken care of. The food was very good and reasonably prices (well for a city centre pub anyway). On the second floor, you can get a nice view of the cathedral.

Visit Two Great Bookshops

I'm a lover of bookstores, so I always look up if there are any located in the places we travel and was chuffed to find there were two very good bookstores in Winchester, worth a visit even for visitors. First is P&G Wells (a suitable English name for a bookstore)

located on the same street at Jane Austen's death house (in fact three doors down). It's a lovely little bookshop that focuses on new titles (and they have new title prices). If secondhand bookstores are more your thing then check out The Winchester Bookshop, located just off the high street in an alley (follow the signs). They have a wide range of secondhand and antiquarian titles. I had one discovery that I will cherish in my library of British books. It's a small little place that is exactly how you imagine a provincial second-hand bookstore to be. Prices were also pretty reasonable. Definitely, stop in.

Military Museums

Winchester is home to six unique military related museums; there is plenty to do and see. With a history dating back to the formation of the British Army, this group of military museums is one of Winchester's hidden gems. The museums feature HorsePower: The Museum of the King's Royal Hussars, Royal Hampshire Regiment Museum, located in Serle's House, Royal Green Jackets (Rifles) Museum, The Gurkha Museum, Museum of the Adjutant General's Corps. Some of the museums are free; some have a small admission fee. If you're interested in British military history, then you definitely want to check these places out.

Winchester City Mill

It's rather odd to find a National Trust property in the middle of a bustling city, but they're not just country houses - they have properties in many different types of places. Winchester City Mill has stood at the heart of the historic city of Winchester – the capital of Kind Alfred's Wessex - since Saxon times. With a history of more than 1,000 years, Winchester City Mill is also the oldest working water mill in the country. A rare surviving example of an urban working corn mill, the City Mill was rebuilt in 1744 and remained in use until the early 20th century. Having entered the care of the National Trust in the late 1920s, the City Mill was restored to full working order in 2004. The mill is open daily and is a great place to start your walk around Winchester.

Shop on the high street

Winchester has a very nice high street - known at The Broadway - with parts that date back centuries. But it's also a modern shopping district with plenty of shops to explore from small traders unique to Winchester to major British chains. It's a fun and atmospheric place to go for a shop - check out the beautiful Winchester Buttercross just across from the West Cornwall Pasty Co.

King Alfred's Statue

Don't forget to stop and say hello to King Alfred himself. There's a beautiful statue located at the end of The Broadway just a little further on from the Guildhall. The heroic statue was designed by Hamo Thornycroft and erected in 1899 to mark one thousand years since Alfred's death. The artists took some artistic license with his work - Alfred looks more like an Arthurian knight than how he actually looked. Leave it to the Victorians to romanticise and take considerable liberties with an important historical figure. It's the middle of a traffic island - so watch your step before you attempt to get close to it.

Getting to Winchester

Winchester is just one hour from London by car, and there is plenty of parking in the city centre - just follow the signs for the car parks. Winchester is also well serviced by trains, and you can get direct trains from London Waterloo. You can also get there by coach via National Express (but this is probably the longest way to get anywhere in England - take the train).

Near Winchester

- Jane Austen's House in Chawton
- Portsmouth Historic Dockyard
- Southampton
- The South Downs Way runs right through the city center
- Beaulieu National Motor Museum
- Mid Hants Steam Heritage Railway (Watercress Line)

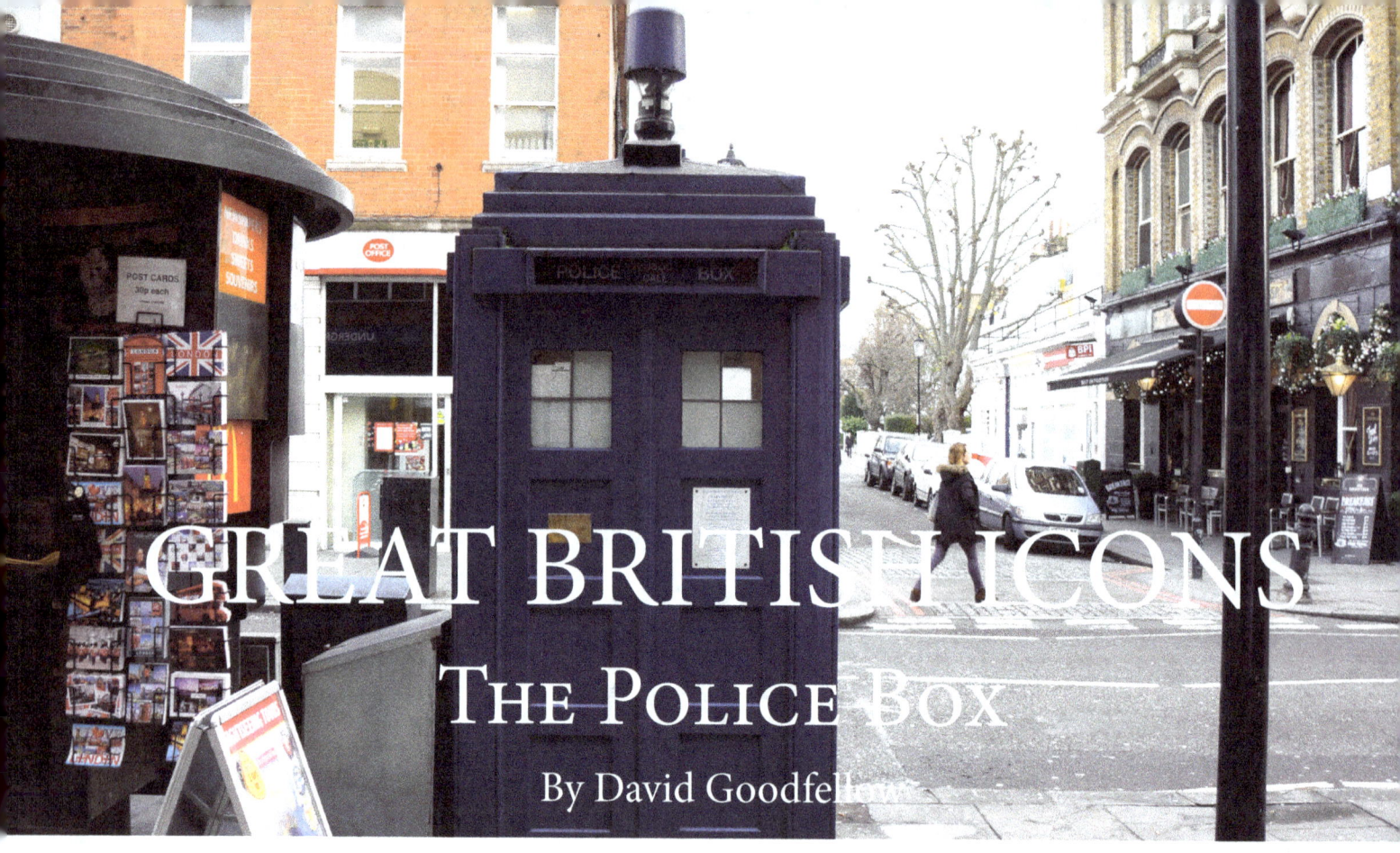

GREAT BRITISH ICONS
The Police Box
By David Goodfellow

The Police Box, now famous for its role in the TV series, "Dr. Who", was first installed in the 1920s in Sunderland, then in London, and soon across the country. In an age without police radios or many public telephones, they provided a way for the public to contact police, ambulance, and fire services, as well as being a rest stop for policemen who patrolled the streets. They were originally red, but became blue in response to the popularity of "Dr. Who". The boxes had a flashing red light on top which could be turned on by the central station to attract policemen nearby. At their peak usage, there were more than 700 boxes in London alone. The introduction of police radios, along with the spread of the telephone and the 999 call system, made the boxes redundant and the last original box was removed in London in 1981. Original boxes can still be seen on the streets of Glasgow and Edinburgh, as well as a replica box outside Earl's Court Underground Station.

It took just a year for Alexander Graham Bell's invention of the telephone to find a role in law enforcement. In 1877, the police department of Albany New York became the first in the world to install a telephone box in the street where the public could contact the police directly. Chicago, Washington, and Boston followed suit in a few years, but it wasn't until 1891 that the first such boxes in the UK were installed in Glasgow. These first boxes were tall, hexagonal and made of cast-iron, like large versions of the post boxes that had become well-known since they were installed across the country in the previous forty years.

The Glasgow boxes had an ingenious mechanism that allowed the central police station to light a gas lamp that was mounted on the top, to signal police in the area. Only policemen and trusted members of the public, who were issued with a special key, could access the telephone inside the box. A newer, rectangular box with electric light was introduced in 1912, but only policemen could use it, to contact the central station.

The north-eastern city of Sunderland was the first place to allow full public access to the box. The Chief Constable, Frederick J. Crawley, installed square wooden boxes there in 1923, which allowed anyone to access police, ambulance, and fire services. Facilities for policemen, including a stool, desk, electric light and a heater were also included in the box, making it a miniature police station. This meant that policemen on the beat – that is, walking the streets - did not have to return to the stations for breaks, so they were able to spend 25% more time actively patrolling. The public telephone and a first-aid kit were on the outside of the box, and only the police had a key for the interior area.

The success of Crawley's innovation led to the adoption of such boxes in other cities, and the first was installed in London in 1928. The London Metropolitan Police Force had the first boxes designed by their own Surveyor and Architect, Gilbert MacKenzie Trench. His first box, installed in 1929, became the prototype for most subsequent boxes that were installed across the city. They were made of concrete, with a wooden door and the public telephone was on the outside. A fire extinguisher was added to the basic interior equipment. There was a red light on the top which could be flashed to attract the attention of police in the vicinity. There were actually three models, with slight differences in design and construction, called Mark 1, 2 and 3. By 1937 a network of 700 boxes was installed across London, including 70 smaller 'police post' boxes with just a telephone, a first-aid kit, and a light.

The success of this system in London led to its introduction in Glasgow and Edinburgh. The Chief Constable in Glasgow was Percy Sillitoe, who subsequently became the director-general of the spy agency MI5. He had 323 boxes of the Mark 1 London design installed across the city during the 1930's. In Edinburgh, a unique design, with neo-classical elements, including corner pillars, was created by the City Architect, Ebenezer J Macrae. Rather than concrete, these boxes were made of cast-iron from Scotland's booming foundries. 86 boxes were in use at their peak.

Police boxes spread across the country, with local variations in each town. Some boxes were combined with letter boxes to a standard Post Office design. During WWII, the black-out laws to protect against German air-raids resulted in a cover being put over the lights, rendering them useless in the eyes of the beat-policemen. Although boxes continued into the 1970's, the introduction of portable radios for each officer made them redundant to police use. The spread of public call-boxes, private phones and the introduction of the 999 system made them unnecessary for the public as well, and they began to be removed.

It is often not realized that the original boxes were painted red until the premiere in 1963 of the

Key Facts

- Originated in America but were widely adopted in the UK
- Provided a rest-stop for policemen on the beat, as well as a telephone for the public
- Changed colour from red to blue after the TV series, "Dr. Who.
- Instantly recognisable image of 20th century London

BBC TV series, "Dr. Who", which featured a blue police box as the TARDIS, a time-travel machine. So popular did the show become that police boxes across the country were re-painted 'TARDIS-blue.' A protracted legal battle between the Metropolitan Police and the BBC over the ownership of the design of the box ended with a surprising victory for the BBC since the box design was seen in other British cities as well as London. The usage of boxes continued to decline, and the last Metropolitan Police Box was removed in 1981.

Sites to Visit

- Although the "Dr. Who" series ended in 1989 (it was later revived in 2005), its image continued, and in 1996 a replica police box was erected outside the Earl's Court Tube station. Instead of a light, it has a CCTV camera mounted on the top.
- A number of original Macrae boxes can still be seen in Edinburgh, including some converted into coffee shops.
- The Civil Defence & Emergency Service Preservation Trust maintain four original boxes in Glasgow.
- There is an original box at the Grampian Transport Museum outside Aberdeen, Scotland. The museum is open daily during the summer.
- There is an original box on the ground of the Metropolitan Police College at Hendon. The grounds are not open to the public, but the determined can see the box from the passing Northern Line Tube, between Colindale and Hendon Central stations.

LOST IN THE POND

By Laurence Brown

Regular readers of this column will recall that in the magazine's second issue, I confidently declared my relationship with America to be over. It was a done deal; the allure of that old flame—the United Kingdom—had proven too strong and all that was needed was for me to let America down gently.

And then, in a period of intense self-reflection, something utterly unexpected occurred: I had a change of heart.

Just as I was hammering out the final revisions to the 'it's-not-you-it's-me' email (this metaphor is getting oddly specific), I took a moment to pause and consider the consequences of my actions. It was at this very moment that my brain decided to transport me back in time to 1993.

Twenty-four years ago—at the age of 12—I had walked into my school's library for the first of only two occasions. I was by no means a shy reader; I just didn't entirely care for the aroma of disinfectant or the stern librarian who, once an hour, sprayed it.

But on this first occasion, nestled between what was probably a 1992 edition of Pears' Cylopedia (a still-circulated British print publication that is apparently either unaware or unphased by the existence of Wikipedia) and Michael Palin's Pole to Pole, I discovered a book that would change my life forever.

This was high praise, by the way, for a book light on plot twists and heavy on mundane geography summaries. But that's precisely what America: An Aerial View was. It detailed, through the use of Aerial photography, the geological splendo(u)r of the United States.

Even for a kid with an inexhaustible thirst for all things American, such a book—not to mention the photographic narrative therein—was hard to come by in pre-Internet Britain. Like the mid-19th century miners referenced in the book's section on California, I had struck gold.

Henceforth, I began to learn all of the state names, memorize the various terrains associated with them, and eventually confront the mountainous challenge of the state capitals.

And then, after all that, the book's return date—having been stamped with trademark venom by the librarian—had arrived. It was time for America: An Aerial View to face one of two fates: 1) go back on the library bookshelf, whereupon it would likely rest, untouched, for what then remained of the twentieth century, or 2) be renewed for a further two months.

No prizes for guessing which option I went with. Only I was not an entirely punctual child; two months soon became two years, which—before I knew it—became two decades, and now 23 years. I accidentally stole the book, is what I'm saying. This fact, of course, has prompted recurring nightmares in which, returning to Heathrow, I am confronted by the librarian—pitchfork in hand—as she heads up a snarling police presence at the arrivals lounge.

But having gathered dust in my parents' spare bedroom, the book recently found its way back into my possession, courtesy of my mum. It was the highest level of promptness the book had known in almost a quarter of a century.

Tearing away the manilla envelope earlier this year, the book's smell emanated from within: not so much that of disinfectant these days, but of my childhood bedroom. The nostalgia quickly came flooding back.

Indeed, with the turn of every page, so did my appreciation for the landscape of America. I'll admit that, amid the bitter political climate that engulfed the nation in 2016, I had allowed myself to forget this side of America. We all did.

It is a land of incredible geological diversity and breathtaking natural terrain. I didn't want to kick America to the curb before I'd realised a childhood ambition to see it. And so, I have set myself the goal—insane though it may be—of visiting all 50 states before the decade is out.

And I'm off to a good start, with pins already pierced into 20 states (though some would argue that layovers at Minneapolis–Saint Paul and Philadelphia International Airports don't count!). But most of these states were nestled up in the north-east, where places are so small it is humanly possible to knock out all nine states in the region in a single day.

The bigger task facing me is the west. Many states beyond the Mississippi River are mind-bogglingly large. In fact, for some perspective, 10 of those states—Alaska, Texas, California, Montana, New Mexico, Arizona, Nevada, Colorado, Oregon, and Wyoming—are each larger than the entire United Kingdom. Remember that the UK is made up of four separate countries.

Beginning in November, my wife and I—now entirely shot of our own vehicle—will conquer a good portion of those states the only way we know how: by train. Traversing America aboard Amtrak's California Zephyr, we will pass through the scenic overtures of the Rocky Mountains and the Sierra Nevada en route to San Francisco.

After four days in the Bay area, we'll then head north via the epically named Coast Starlight to Seattle, being sure to mingle with artists and hipsters in the city of Portland along the way.

Eventually, once we've frequented every single coffee shop in Seattle and ceased gawping at Mount Rainier, we will make the potentially treacherous—and therefore exhilarating—journey back to Chicago via Idaho, Montana, North Dakota, Minnesota, and Wisconsin.

In all, our journey will take in ten new states, leaving a mere twenty to cover in the remaining two years. I suppose, considering that it has taken me since 1990 to achieve that precise number, an uphill challenge lies ahead (especially in the Rockies!). But, having announced my intentions to not only the readers of this eminent magazine but also subscribers of my blog's YouTube channel, I have no choice but to remain accountable and to meet that very challenge.

If only I'd been blessed with such motivating factors all those years ago, when America: An Aerial View's return date came and went. Then again, had that been so, I probably wouldn't be undertaking this 50-state challenge at all. The moral of the story, then, is that it pays to fear librarians.

Laurence is a British writer and humorist who lives in the United States. He also hosts the popular web series, Lost in the Pond on YouTube. He has an infuriating habit of taking America to task by pointing out how things are done in the UK. He really needs to stop this behavio(u)r. It's anti-American.

WILLIAM III

William and Mary and the Glorious Revolution

William and Mary's marriage and joint reign over England, Scotland and Ireland were the product of lengthy political machinations. Parliament was in agreement that King James II, Mary's father, had to go and what better solution than to join the protestant cousins, William and Mary, in holy matrimony, have William invade England and place the crown on Mary's head? Mary insisted on a co-regency but the Bill of Rights that followed, an important document that hugely limited the sovereign's power over tax, legislation, the military and the treasury, may have been more than she bargained for. William spent eight months out of every twelve fighting a war with France and survived two Jacobite attempts to overthrow him, but his reign was short at just 13 years. Mary died after just five years on the throne and as she died childless, the couple had failed to begin a dynasty of their own, and the crown was passed promptly to Mary's sister, Anne upon William's death.

Both William and Mary's childhoods were sadly lacking in parental influence. William's father, William II, died a week before he was born meaning William was the Sovereign Prince of Orange from the moment of his birth. Mary also grew up motherless from the age of ten and was separated from her father James, then Duke of York, because it was thought imperative that Mary remain a Protestant while James was an open and dedicated Catholic.

In 1677, William and Mary were married despite the fact that they were first cousins. Mary was William's mother's niece and the daughter of his maternal uncle, James, Duke of York. The circumstances of William and Marys' succession to the English throne were unconventional, to say the least. King James II of England and II of Ireland, and VII of Scotland, Mary's father, was overthrown and militarily defeated in the so-called Glorious Revolution of 1688 by a union of English Parliamentarians led by William III of Orange who just happened to be Mary's husband.

James II and the other Stuart kings who came before him were accused by Parliament of repeated and gross abuses of their sovereign power. Several long centuries of conflict between the parliament and the crown came to a head in 1688 as the question of succession and, most-importantly, the religion of the next king or queen came into

Key Facts

- William, son of William II of Orange, was born on 14 November 1650 (Georgian Calendar) at The Hague. Mary, the eldest daughter of King James II, was born on the 30 April 1662 at St. James' Palace.
- William III and Mary II succeeded as the King of England and Ireland and Queen of England and Ireland on 13 February 1689.
- William and Mary were married on 4 November 1677 in London. William was 27 at the time and Mary was 15.
- William died on 8 March 1702, having reigned in England for thirteen years. Mary died on the 28 December 1694, having reigned just five years.

focus. William of Orange's successful invasion of England forced King James II to flee to France and allowed Parliament to depose him on the grounds of desertion.

Despite the fact that James II had an infant son, James Francis Edward, who should have succeeded him by hereditary principle, it was Mary to whom the English throne was offered by parliament. This was not an oversight but a tactical move by parliament who wanted to restrict the succession to a Protestant line, ensuring an end to the idea that England may be restored to Roman Catholicism. To make it official, William and Mary accepted a Parliamentary Act of Settlement that meant their title to the throne was only valid by an act of Parliament.

Although William had militarily defeated James II and invaded England, Mary was senior to her husband in her claim on the English throne and could have reigned independently. However, her insistence that she wished to resign her rights altogether to William resulted in Parliament offering the crown to the couple jointly as king and queen regnant.

The English Bill of Rights (1689) was drawn up by Parliament and signed by William and Mary in 1689. The bill was conceived to ensure that the power of the monarchy would be, in the future, limited and that Parliament could function

free from royal interference. Importantly the bill reaffirmed Parliament's control of taxation and legislation in England meaning the Sovereign was forbidden from levying taxes without Parliamentary consent or interfering with laws already passed by Parliament. The royal court was abolished, and the proper court was forbidden from imposing cruel punishments or excessive bail. Freedom of speech was to be upheld, and the sovereign was banned from having anything to do with elections or from maintaining their own army. Finally, Parliament put an end to the monarchy's use of England's treasury as a personal piggy bank and tightened control over the sovereign's expenditure.

This magnificent document inspired the English colonists in the Thirteen Colonies that would later become part of the United States of America, to revolt against King James II and his stance on colonial government. Revolts occurred in New York, Massachusetts, and Maryland in 1689.

One of the main factors that motivated William's marriage to Mary and the seizing of the English throne was to embroil the English in the ongoing war between the Netherlands and Louis XIV of France. The Dutch and the English joined the coalition against France during the Nine Years War, hoping to limit France's expansion in Europe. This long and costly war came to an end in 1697 with The Peace of Rijswijk treaty. William immediately formed an alliance with England, Holland, and Austria in an attempt to prevent the France and Spain from uniting. This move led to the 'War of the Spanish Succession.'

Soon after Mary and William's wedding Mary had become pregnant but miscarried and due to a later illness was unable to give birth to a child. In 1694 Mary died of smallpox, aged just 32 years and childless. With Mary dead William's popularity with the English public dwindled further. Already criticised for his conflict with France which was a venture more beneficial to the Netherlands than England, William now became a target for more Jacobite plots. William and Mary had already fought two Jacobite rebellions in 1689. Scottish Jacobites defeated the Scottish army at Killiekrankie and James II fought with French troops in Londonderry. William's navy defeated James' and he led an English army to victory at the Battle of the Boyne in 1690.

In 1701, James II died, and Louis XIV recognised his son, James, Duke of York, the Catholic son who had been skipped in the succession for Mary, as King of England. This move created a surge in popularity for William's war with France with many patriots and politicians rallying to protect their nation and its sovereign. Just a year later though, on the 8th March 1702, William died of bacterial pneumonia following a fall whilst riding at Hampton Court. It was Mary's younger sister Anne's turn to take to the throne.

Legacy Today

The most significant event of William and Mary's reign was the signing of the English Bill of Rights in 1689. This bill dramatically increased the English Parliament's influence and ended many centuries of hostility between parliament and the crown. It also comforted a nation of Protestants who were now satisfied that England would not be returned to Roman Catholicism and inspired English colonists in the Thirteen Colonies to make their first loud steps towards American Independence. William's victory over James II at the Battle of the Boyne ensured the Protestant faith kept its hold in Britain and his war with France, although costly and beneficial to his native Netherlands, did put a stop to Catholic Louis XIV's ambitions to expand his territory.

Film & TV Appearances

William III

- The League of Gentlemen's Apocalypse (2005)
- Blood Royal: William the Conqueror (1990) TV play
- Orlando (1992)
- Peter the Great (1986) TV series
- The First Churchills (1969)
- Against All Flags (1952)
- Captain Kidd (1945)
- The Black Tulip (1937)

Mary II

- The League of Gentlemen's Apocalypse (2005)
- England, My England (1995)
- Orlando (1992)
- The First Churchills (1969)

Further Research

- Waller, Maureen (2006). Sovereign Ladies: The Six Reigning Queens of England
- Van der Kiste, John (2003) William and Mary
- Van der Zee, Henri and Barbara. William and Mary (1973)
- Baxter, Stephen B, William III and the Defense of European Liberty, 1650–1702 (1966)
- Chapman, Hester W., Mary II: Queen of England (1953)

Locations to Visit

- Mary II was born at St James's Palace, died at Kensington Palace, and is buried at Westminster Abbey.
- William III was born at Binnenhof, The Hague, died at Kensington Palace and is buried at Westminster Abbey.
- William and Mary lived primarily between their palaces at Whitehall and Kensington in London.

MILTON ABBAS
One of the First Planned Communities in England
By Jonathan Thomas

Joseph Damer, Lord Milton, was by all accounts an unpleasant man. All he wanted was solitude and to be left alone. So much so that he had an entire village demolished and relocated to improve the view from his house. Out of spite he bought and threw away the local church bells when they sounded after a court case where he was the loser (the bells were celebrating something else). He hated children and used an act of parliament to relocate a grammar school (he claimed the boys kept stealing his apple).

But yet we have him to thank for the existence of Milton Abbas (pronounced abbess), which in historical context is a bit of a strange place. When we think of a planned community, we think of neat and tidy American suburb with grid streets and cul-de-sacs galore. There's nothing soulful about it. Most towns and villages in England grew organically without a plan, order was not the default, and you can tell just by looking at a map of any place in England, it's a mess. Yet the village of Milton Abbas in Dorset is a planned community, and it's beautiful. It's a historical quirk, that was built in the 1700s and this past spring we had a chance to visit.

The original village of Milton Abbas, which was actually called Middleton, was a thriving market town that few up around Milton Abbey, at one point a Benedictine monastery and later on a private estate after the dissolution of the monasteries in 1539. Middleton's history goes back more than 1,000 years when the abbey was founded by the Anglo-Saxon King Athelstan. This combination of a private estate being essentially next to a village was a source of continued irritation for the landowners until Joseph Damer came along. Damer acquired the estate in 1752 after a series of owners.

According to a chronicle of local history that I picked up during our visit (£2.50 in the Abbey honesty shop), the dispute began with an apple tree. Or rather the Grammar School established in 1521 that was near the apple tree. As boy are known to be rather rambunctious, they would steal apples and other vegetables from Damer's private garden when they went to school. Damer repeatedly tried to close the school but was unsuccessful until finally getting an Act of Parliament to move the school to Blandford Forum (you have to really hate something to get Parliament to do something about it).

Despite this small victory, Damer had had enough and decided that the views of his Capability

Brown designed garden could be substantially improved if the village was to be demolished and relocated out of his direct view. No more pesky kids stealing his apples and no villagers to cause him trouble. The plan started in secret. As leases to properties in the village came up for renewal, he would not renew them and force the people to leave. Eventually, everyone caught on to what he was doing, and locals began to resist.

Damer claimed that he was really doing them all a favor as the village was prone to occasional flooding and moving would allow them to properly drain the local stream into a new lake which would conveniently make his estate prettier. Since Damer was the landowner and had all the power, the villagers really had no choice in the matter.

So, a new village was laid out in the next valley. The new village of Milton Abbas would have all the amenities of the old one except that all the cottages would look exactly the same. The thatched cottages were designed by Sir William Chambers, who worked with Capability Brown on the gardens surrounding Milton Abbey. Once the old village was demolished, there was no trace of it left on the neatly sculpted grounds of Milton Abbey. Much of the remains are at the bottom of the lake that was created by Capability Brown (though the lake was never 'finished' it's only a shadow of it's original planned size).

Most of the thatched cottages are the same size and shape. They're what the English call semi-detached, or two houses sharing the same frame (a duplex basically). Each side of the house has two rooms downstairs and two rooms upstairs. The central door in the front would lead to a small hallway with two front doors to each adjoining houses. This arrangement was not permanent, many of the houses now have been knocked through and are now one residence.

The village had everything a town of its size would need to function. At one point there was a brewery, a doctor's surgery, a pub, a workhouse, post office, school, bank, church and even a slaughterhouse. The nicest house in the village is the Old Vicarage, which is where the local priest used to live (it's now a private home) and it does not share the look of the other thatched cottages. There are also almshouses in the village, which are still in use today as homes for the elderly in the village (places are reserved for people who spent their whole life in the village).

Time marches on and the village and changed with it. When this 'model village' was built, most of the inhabitants worked in the surrounding estate in agriculture. Nowadays, not a single person works in agriculture, and most people work in the surrounding communities or commute to local cities such as Dorchester or Blandford Forum. There's still a local pub, but the brewery and most of the other business needed by a Georgian village are gone. All that's left is a small village shop offering essential provisions and postal services.

Despite the trauma of being removed from their homes, many of which had lived there for generations, the villagers adapted to their new home. It didn't hurt that many of the cottages were of a more modern standard than what they were used to so the new village was much nice than what they were used to. The current villagers are very proud of their little community. All the houses are currently lived in. Most recognize that there's a bit of a blight to their lovely village, cars upon cars, destroy the lines and nice views the village could present if they weren't there.

The day we visited was a brisk late February day. It was overcast, and clearly, we were not seeing the village at its best. There was a strong wind, the layout of the valley turns it into a wind tunnel, thankfully it's at your back as you explore the village. But when you head back, uphill I should add, the wind is pushing against you as you walk. The village was active; there was the sound of hammers and scaffolding be erected as builders were preparing to renovate one of the cottages, which are all in different states of condition. Some are immaculate, some have seen better days. All the cottages are privately owned today as are the rest of the properties in the village after it was sold off in 1932 by the Hambro family. One owner was clearly the wisteria from the front of his. All were friendly and waved hello as we walked through the town.

There's not much to see there other than the village itself. We popped into the local church; there was a sign outside indicating there was a DVD on show about the history of the village. The church was lovely for a small English village church. But the DVD didn't work despite repeatedly repeating the steps in the directions. I had directions for a walk that takes you from the new village, along the lake, and to Milton Abbey, then back around to see the

Clockwise from Top Left: Cottage, Almshouses, Post Office and Village Shop, Milton Abbey

whole village. The walk was easy to follow. There's only one 'street' in the village. Sidewalks were not in the original plan, so you must walk along the street. Which is fine, there's not much traffic going through the village; it's not on a main road.

We made our way to Milton Abbey, it's about a mile walk, on flat terrain so it's not too strenuous. The path takes you along the lake and the back garden of a lovely house located on the hills above. The Abbey is now a well-known girls school. It's not a place that's open to the public.

After the dissolution of the monasteries, the monastic buildings were demolished and a great stately home was built, which is what makes up the bulk of the school now. The Abbey and its ground were bought for a song by Sir John Tregonwell. Tregonwell was one of the lawyers that helped secure Henry VIII's divorce. So, you can clearly see some dodgy dealings went on here. The Tregonwell family held on to the place for a few centuries then went through a series of owners, including our friend Damer above, ending with the Hambro family who sold the lot in 1932. The girls' school was founded in 1953 and continues to operate today.

We visited on a weekday, so classes were in session. However, we did not see any students. Visitors are only permitted up the path that leads directly to the Abbey doors; they're not allowed to wander the grounds. Most of the landscape grounds have been taken over by a Golf Course for the girls who attend the school (the Golfers at the school are apparently quite good). The Abbey itself is surrounded by the former house and other buildings needed for a functioning school.

The grounds were very quiet, and it was rather like visiting a Stately Home property and having the place to yourself. The doors to the Abbey are open to visitors during 'normal' visiting hours, and it's quite something to unlatch the big metal handle and let yourself through the big wooden doors. It's like stepping onto a movie set. The Abbey is a very fine building. It's currently used at the school's church, but there was no one inside when we visited. We were literally the only people alive in the place. There are, however, plenty of dead people buried inside the Abbey including the various former

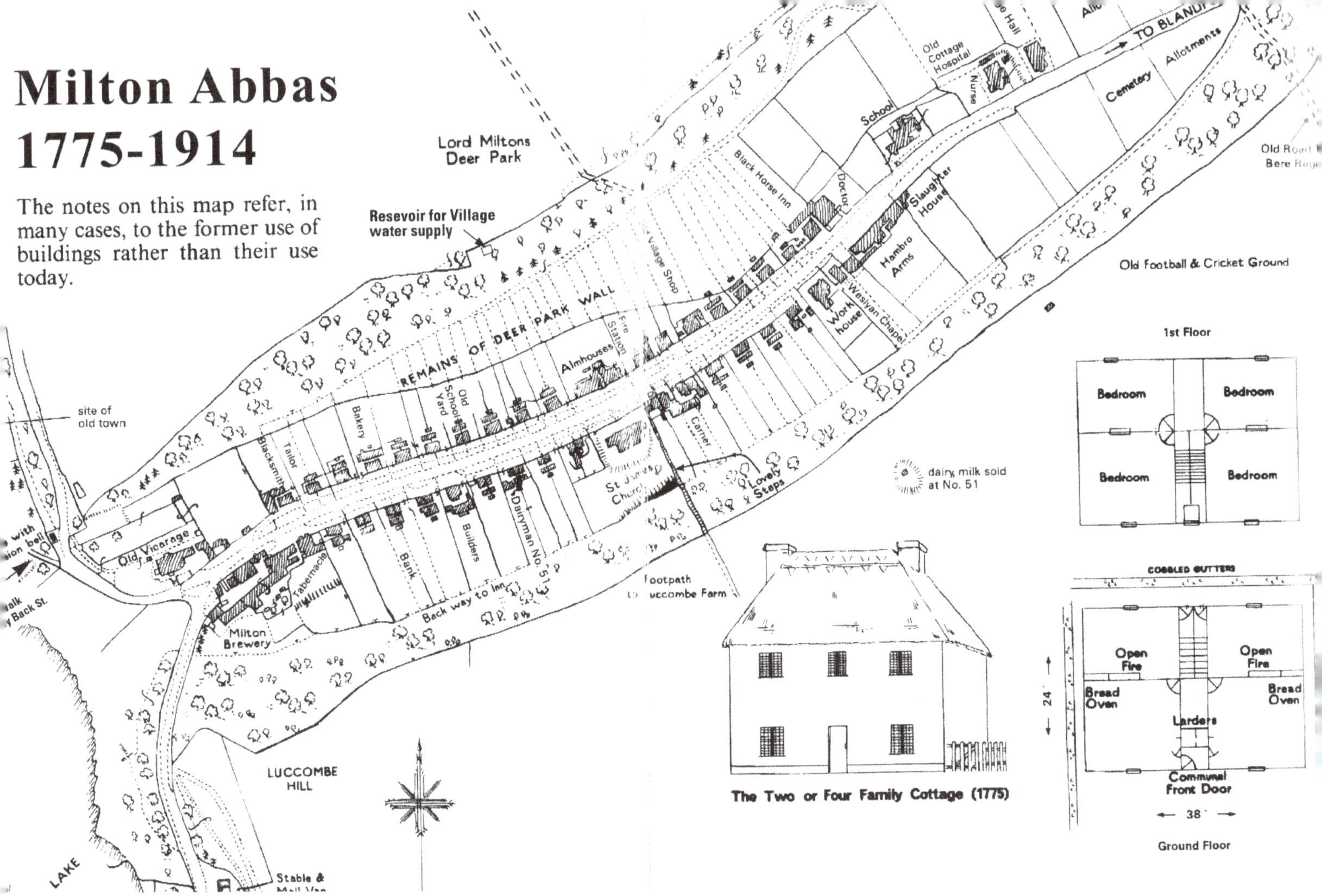

Milton Abbas 1775-1914

The notes on this map refer, in many cases, to the former use of buildings rather than their use today.

Map of the Village Plan

owners of the estate (including Lord Damer). The Abbey is not particularly remarkable as Abbey's go, but it's still a stunning building - and with bits of it almost 1,000 years old, you can hear the echoes of history in the place. It was a treat to have such a magnificent building completely to ourselves.

Milton Abbas may have been created to fulfill the desires of a greedy landowner seeking to get away from his tenants, but the result is a beautiful time capsule of thatched cottages that is a thriving village. It's places like this that make me love England, and I was very happy to visit and will do so again, perhaps when they have their next village fair.

If you go

You will need a car to get to Milton Abbas. Public Transportation is not a reliable way to get there. You could perhaps take a train in Dorchester and then take a taxi. But a car is really required. You can park on the main street, there's plenty of parking (as you see by the legions of cars ruining the view). We highly recommend doing the walk from the village to the Abbey. Just stick to the path as the school is not open to the public. You can see the whole place and do the walk in 2-3 hours. It's a great stop on the way to somewhere else in Dorset. There's nowhere to stay in the village, it's very much a living village and not really on the tourist trail. So, have a stop, enjoy the views and go on our way.

Great British Art - The Battle of Trafalgar by JMW Turner

This is considered Turner's most controversial painting. In 1822, JMW Turner created the large-scale oil painting of The Battle of Trafalgar that took place on 21 October 1805. King George IV commissioned this work to be part of a series of works in St. James Palace to decorate three state reception rooms and link the Hanoverian dynasty with military success. This work was Turner's only royal commission. Rather than paint any one piece of the battle, he combined several recorded events into one scene. So as a piece of history, the painting is not accurate. Turner did his homework, however, completing several sketches of the Victory herself. On delivery in 1824, the painting provoked court criticism for its non-chronological approach to Nelson's victory, and its powerful allusions to the blood price of Britain's triumph, at Trafalgar and more generally in becoming the world's dominant sea power. It's currently on display at the National Maritime Museum in Greenwich.

THIS ENGLISH LIFE
My First Passport
By Erin Moore

On the way to my son's play group, in Coram's Fields near Russell Square, we get a history lesson. The park was the original site of the Foundling Hospital, established in 1739 by Captain Thomas Coram to help the many homeless and abandoned children living on the streets of London. Today such a childhood would be called Dickensian, but it wasn't until 1837 that Charles Dickens, then only 25 himself, would publish Oliver Twist. Life went on being hard for children in this part of London for a very long time, and Dickens wouldn't live to see the site become the playground it is today, full of laughing and well-fed faces.

Right across from Coram's Fields is the site of a more personal history: International Hall, the dormitory where, age 20, I arrived as a student knowing no one. I was not allowed into Coram's Fields because only people with children may enter. If you'd told me then that one day I would push my 2-year-old on the swings there, I wouldn't have believed a word. Before that trip, like the majority of Americans, I didn't even have a passport. When I was a kid growing up in the Florida Keys, a trip to Disney's Epcot Center was the closest thing we had to foreign travel.

My beloved grandmother, Nana, was the first person who let me know there was an England. She had spent several years on a U.S. Air Force base in the Cotswolds, and she had a collection of Toby jugs and a lingering love for the British Royal Family. It was probably her fault that I dragged my mother out of bed at 4 a.m. to watch the Princess Diana's wedding to Prince Charles on TV. A few years later, Nana gave me a pop-up book with pictures of Charles and Diana and their baby sons, and we used to look at it together. Many years later I would the same book displayed for ironic effect in the home of a Cambridge, Massachusetts intellectual. But Nana and I were completely earnest in our obsession.

My grandmother would have loved the books I read to my children now: in addition to Nancy Drew, my daughter loves Enid Blyton's boarding school books and the Famous Five. My son loves Mo Willems and Dr. Seuss, but he is also into anything by Julia Donaldson (The Gruffalo) and John Ryan's Captain Pugwash series. I'm not sure if Nana ever read Thomas Hardy, Jane Austen, or Charles Dickens, but it was because of her that I sought them out. When I got to college, a survey course in British literature called to me like nothing else. Could the London of my imagination, informed only by books, possibly measure up in real life? I had to see it. How would my sentimental (much less academic) education be complete otherwise?

It occurred to me one day, late in my freshman year, that while I had come quite far from home, I was unlikely to get any further without serious machinations. When Europeans roll their eyes that only something like 36% of Americans have passports, I remind them that America is a huge country. It would take my family 8 or 9 hours in the car to get to the middle of Florida from where we lived. If we wanted to leave the state, it was more like 14 hours. We'd be in Georgia then, which is a lovely place but not meaningfully different from northern Florida. The only families we knew who made pilgrimages to Europe did so because they had family living there. Plane tickets were expensive. Then it came to me: A junior year abroad would be the perfect way to see something more of the world.

First passport in hand, I was accepted to King's College London and arrived at International Hall with my brand new suitcase and a more or less sensible haircut and was swept immediately into a polyglot spree of undergraduates from all over Europe. The dorm was run down, but clean, and the food was appalling, but the beer was cheap. We felt right at home.

I spent the first few weeks acquainting myself with literary London. I went to the Charles Dickens Museum in Doughty Street, just a couple of blocks from my dormitory (and managed to get lost on the way home). I went to Thomas Carlyle's house in Cheyne Row. I went to the British Museum and the Tate Britain, and I read every blue plaque along the way. I was an A+ student of the Tube and soon found everything I needed: a hairdryer from Argos (like a tiny version of Service Merchandise—remember that place?); a duvet cover from Habitat; stacks and stacks of novels and the Complete Works of Shakespeare from Foyles; a much edgier haircut from the hairdressing students at Tony and Guy; membership at the student union; and a regular sandwich shop where they tolerated my American approach to ordering.

Before I knew it, I had stopped looking for other people's London and started finding my own, which I remember like a series of snapshots from an old scrapbook: the Slug and Lettuce, a pub in Islington where I learned to drink wine but avoid the "large" glasses which contain half a bottle; an all-night vigil outside the Almeida theatre for cheap tickets to Ivanov starring dreamy Ralph Fiennes (my friend and I were the only ones in the queue who were not being paid to be there, but we got the tickets and sat rapt in the balcony not noticing RF's bald spot); the dusty and perfect used bookshops in Charing Cross Road where 50p was a lot of money; the bar in Covent Garden where my classmates introduced me to Guinness and Black (Guinness with a purple-hued head of blackcurrant cordial: possibly why I cannot abide blackcurrant flavored anything to this day); my first and only cigarette on a freezing night near Kings Cross, a place we had been warned to stay away from for a reason, and far from the tourist magnet it would become; the NHS surgery where I went for the terrible case of bronchitis that resulted; teeming thrift shops in Brixton; the tiny phone booth in the hall from which I called my parents every two weeks; the chilly library where the internet was so glacial it took an hour to send an email; the offices of my professors where I sat knee-to-knee with British students in tutorials, trying (failing) not to speak first; the long afternoons of reading in the fortress of Senate House (the imposing model for the Ministry of Truth in George Orwell's 1984; Brunswick Centre then: a scrubby concrete shopping mall, half empty but for an off-license and an Iceland and the perfect setting for a dystopian novel (now, a bucolic middle class wonderland with a water feature, a Waitrose, a Carluccio's, and an art house cinema). It was nothing like Epcot.

I'm so grateful for every one of those experiences. Some of my friends who've hit 40 talk about having the Talking Heads "this is not my beautiful house" moment, when "you may ask yourself, 'how did I get here?'" They feel disoriented—as if they turned around one day and there was this husband, these kids, this life, and it just sort of happened to them without their explicit agency. Like the heroine in a Thomas Hardy novel, happy or not thanks to the unseen hand of fate.

During my year in London, I stopped believing in that kind of story. I got into the Modernists instead, found Virginia Woolf's Mrs. Dalloway and decided

to buy my own flowers. Coming here all alone—and learning that such things were possible—bolstered my courage to follow my curiosity. It was the first step on the path to living here permanently, in the sort of place I used to admire from outside at night.

"My" London today is the Georgian house in Islington where my husband and I live with our kids and our books and our cat; the Nordic Bakery, whose cinnamon scent somehow makes it easier to concentrate on work (but the chocolate oatmeal cookies make it harder); Daunt Books in Marylebone High Street, where we had a book launch party for That's Not English and where my kids can always talk me into buying just one more; the corner shop Henry always points out on the way home with a hopeful, "Loclit buttons, Mama?"; Bentley's Oyster Bar, where Nigel Slater took me for dinner when we were working on the U.S. edition of his memoir, Toast, and where my oyster-guzzling daughter is not just welcome, but loved; Radnor Mews, where we took our firstborn home from the hospital and where we still get invited to the best street parties, even though we don't live there anymore; Hyde Park, where I used to recognize all the runners; University Hospital, where Anne was born; and the Portland Hospital where she and Tom visited me and newborn Henry. Sometimes I worry about how small my London has become, and it's true that I spend most days within 2 miles of home, but life is so much richer in relationships than it was 20 years ago, and I'm reminded it's really people—not places or things—that make a home.

I walk Henry in his pushchair past my old dormitory every week now. We're allowed in Coram's Fields, thanks to him. In addition to the play group, it has a sand pit, a petting zoo, a zip-line, a fountain and a coffee kiosk that's never open as early as a parent would wish. I look forward to taking Henry and his sister to Epcot when they are old enough to understand the world it gave me before I had been anywhere to write home about. And I hope one day they will want to read the books that are the reasons why they are here: souvenirs of where I've been, as well as inspiration to keep exploring. Nana would be proud.

About the Author

Erin Moore is an American who has been living in London for 10 years. Her book, That's Not English: Britishisms, Americanisms and What Our English Says About Us, is available on amazon.com.

GREAT BRITISH QUESTIONS

Your burning questions about Britain answered truthfully.

By The Anonymous Anglophile

What are these concession things I see when paying admissions to attractions in England? - Anglotopia Facebook Page Follower

On the most basic level, a concession is a discount on the admission. The equivalent in the USA would be a Senior Discount or a Student Discount. Instead of having a ton of different categories, the British have one: concessions. If you're in a class that qualifies, i.e., a student, elderly person, unemployed or disabled, you can get the concession price. Often you have to prove your right to get the concession.

I am heading back to England for three weeks later this month. All of my major costs are already paid. I have been thinking about getting a pre-paid currency card loaded in GBP for incidental purchases of food, shopping, etc. However, I've been reading tonight that there are many fees to consider and assorted tricks that cost the cardholder dearly. So, now I'm thinking I should just use my credit card (no foreign transaction fees) and settle the bill when I get home. Since you have just returned, I would appreciate any guidance you would care to offer. - Diane via Email

Good question. Yes, those cards can have lots of fees as that's how they make money and the exchange rates they offer aren't great. Also, if there are issues using the card, it's not easy to get your money back out (and you have to take their exchange rate offer, however bad) because it's not a traditional bank account. I would recommend buying hard currency from somewhere like http://foreignmoney.com (tell them Anglotopia sent you) and using your credit cards since you don't have foreign transaction fees.

That's what has worked for us. I have two credit cards we use on trips (one which has a chip, which helps). Also, make sure your credit card doesn't charge foreign transaction fees, those can add up!

What's the difference between High Tea, Afternoon Tea, etc? - Anonymous Tea Lover

This one can be really confusing. So, here are the basic definitions.

Elevensies - Late morning snack and cup of tea (second breakfast).

Afternoon Tea - A Formal meal where one sits down with cucumber sandwiches, pastries, and fine tea. Usually in a hotel or restaurant around 4 p.m.

High Tea - Less formal than afternoon Tea - usually a late afternoon meal after work but before proper dinner.

Cream Tea - A simpler tea service consisting of tea, scones, clotted cream, marmalade or lemon curd.

Royale Tea - Tea service with champagne or sherry at the end.

Celebration Tea - An afternoon tea service where a cake is served for a special occasion.

Undoubtedly, the British will come up with a completely new version of tea after we've gone to press.

Have a burning question about British travel or Culture? Send it to info@anglotopia.net and we'll get it answered for you! You can also mail a letter using the addresss listed at the front of the magazine.

THE GREAT SMOG OF 1952

The 'Pea-souper' That Kill Thousands and Changes Environmental Laws

By John Rabon

As Christmas drew near in London in 1952, a strange phenomenon like something out of a Quartermass story became all too real for the city's residents. Under a perfect set of conditions, a combination of air pollution and fog combined into one of the worst ecological disasters of the 20th Century. It only lasted five days, but by the time it was through, the Great Smog would be responsible for injuring approximately 200,000 people and killing 12,000. Recently depicted in the original Netflix series The Crown, the smog was an even worse event for London than what was depicted on screen.

The first instances of smog were a result of the coal furnaces that began to appear in the 19th Century as a result of the Industrial Revolution. The smoke and coal ash could be so thick at this time that it was known to change the colour of buildings and even turned 10 Downing Street's bricks from yellow to black. People became so used to the colour that the building's bricks were later painted black to maintain the look. The term "smog" would not come to be used to describe this natural and man-made phenomenon until Dr. Henry Antoine Des Veoux's paper "Smoke and Fog," presented in 1905 at a meeting of the Public Health Congress.

The smog that befell London had two root causes: man-made coal smoke and perfect weather conditions. For weeks prior to the event, the city had experienced an unusual cold snap and businesses, and residents alike burned even more coal to keep warm. Post-war coal was notoriously low-grade with a higher sulphur content (higher quality coal at the time was exported), which in turn added to the sulphur dioxide in the smoke that went up the chimneys and into the London air. In addition to the smoke released from homes and offices, the coal-burning furnaces of factories and major power plants in Battersea, Fulham, Bankside, and Kingston Upon Thames contributed even more pollution. The Met Office figures that, during the smog event, coal burning released 1,000 tonnes of smoke particles, 2,000 tonnes of carbon dioxide, 140 tonnes of hydrochloric acid, 14 tonnes of fluorine compounds, and 370 tonnes of sulphur dioxide.

While this sounds bad on its own, the weather in London during that first week of December made for deadly conditions that would trap all those pollutants within the city. Dr. Renyi Zhang at Texas A&M University in the US, doing a study

of similar effects in Chinese cities, discovered that "under naturally foggy conditions, sulfate will build up inside water droplets due to chemical reactions between sulfur dioxide and nitrogen dioxide." The sulfate then makes the water particles in a fog denser as well as toxic, contributing to even hazier conditions than normal and transforming the water vapor into a deadly inhalant. In the midst of this cold weather, a high-pressure system became stuck over the city due to an anticyclone. This anticyclone and the lack of wind that would ordinarily move these systems along created a temperature inversion wherein the warm air 1,000 feet above London kept cooler air at ground level. The result of the inversion was then to keep the smoke closer to the ground, where the sulphate particles clung to London's fog.

Londoners were pretty used to fog, but as it began to roll in on 5 December 1952, this fog slowly began to show that it was something different and dangerous. The sulphur combined with the water particles in the smog to give it a yellow-ish black colour, leading the citizens to dub it a "pea-souper," but no one on that first day could have known how deadly this fog would become. Trapped under the warm air, the smog became thicker to the point where people couldn't see across the street and some others in East London reported that they couldn't even see their own feet. Visibility at its poorest was done to one foot and it made driving and simply cross the street practically impossible. In less than a day, London was effectively shut down.

London transport stopped completely aside

from the Underground since buses couldn't see where they were going (making the death of Churchill's fictional secretary one the series' historical liberties). Outdoor sporting events ceased, and indoor events were cancelled as the smoke was able to creep into buildings and reduce the visibility of the stage or cinema screen. The only sporting event that was carried out was the cross-country race between Oxford and Cambridge at Wimbledon Common, though it required track marshals to shout verbal directions at the runners to keep them on the course. Authorities told parents to keep their children away from school since they were concerned about the kids getting lost. Ambulance service was halted as well, and those afflicted by the smog were forced to transport themselves to hospitals. The visibility also increased crime as some Londoners took the opportunity to loot closed stores and at least one death was linked to the smog, not because of the cloud's poisonous effects, but because it concealed the stabbing of a sixteen-year-old-girl.

The real deadliness of the smog was not apparent at the beginning of the event. Some of the first casualties were actually birds who got lost in the smog and crashed into buildings. At Earl's Court, eleven heifers choked to death at the Smithfield Show, forcing the remaining livestock owners to quickly fashion crude gas masks out of grain sacks soaked in whiskey. Sadly, this event was buried in a story on page 9 of the paper, but as the smog accumulated to the level that it began to affect humans, nearly everyone began to take it more seriously.

Breathing in the air was equivalent to inhaling acid rain, and those most susceptible were children, the elderly, and persons who already had difficulty breathing. Inhaling smog in any capacity has been found to be linked to everything from minor pains (caused by irritation of the lungs) to lung cancer. In fact, some doctors today believe that many cases of asthma in London during the 1950s were a result of young children and unborn babies being exposed to the sulphur. A study published in the American Journal of Respiratory and Critical Care Medicine found that the Great Smog was responsible for thousands of cases of asthma and that the rate of the condition was 20% more likely in those children and babies born or living in London during that time than outside the city.

It wasn't long before the city's hospitals were inundated by the affected. The death rate in London's East End multiplied by nine, while overall deaths from bronchitis and pneumonia increased by a factor of seven. Even so, the serious health problems presented by the smog were not apparent to the average Londoner until florists began to experience a lack of inventory and undertakers started running out of coffins. Despite all this, there was no great panic or rush on the hospitals as depicted in The Crown. One doctor reported that "there was no sense of drama or emergency." It appears that no real precautions were taken to limit exposure beyond what has already been mentioned, and the true effects of the of the Great Smog were not revealed until a total count of the dead was made. Initial estimates put the figure at 4,000 and rose steadily to 12,000, most of which were due to exacerbation of pre-existing respiratory conditions.

The little reaction from the public was mirrored by their leaders. Whereas the Crown portrays Winston Churchill and his ministers as unresponsive to an increasing public health threat, newspapers from the time seem to focus more on the fog itself and its effects rather than trying to put the blame on anyone in Parliament or Whitehall. Additionally, there isn't much evidence to suggest that the government could have foreseen the fog or its effects before it hit the city. While Harold Macmillan had once called for a committee to be formed to study the effects of air pollution, ultimately nothing came of it before the Great Smog struck in December 1952. Government action would not come for some time after the fog lifted.

The end of the Great Smog would come on 9 December 1952 when a cold wind blew into London from the west and moved the sulphuric cloud out to the North Sea, where it dissipated. Even though the cause of the disaster was gone, the lingering effects caused the death toll to rise to the full 12,000, and the mortality rate remained higher than average through the summer of 1953. While the government initially took no action in the wake of the smog, the London County Council was not so slow to respond and produced its own report in January 1953 that detailed the results of the smog upon the city and its residents. In the same year, doctors began urging Londoners to guard themselves against future events by protecting their lungs with gauze folded into a six-layer mask covering their mouth and nose. However, amidst renewed calls for parliamentary action, Macmillan, then Minister for Housing and Local Government, felt that no "further legislation [was] needed."

It was then under mounting pressure from the LCC and London MPs that the government finally launched its inquiry with a committee led by Sir Hugh Beaver in August 1953. The committee was tasked with investigating the problem of air pollution in general, but it spent its initial months looking into the cause and results of the Great Smog. The committee published its interim report four months later in December, which concluded that domestic coal burning produced twice as much smoke as the city's industries and released the smoke at a lower altitude than the tall chimneys of the power plants and factories. The report also recommended some of the first alternative energy measures, namely in suggesting that smokeless fuels be used in periods in which smog was more likely. Additionally, it recommended that the Meteorological Office put out a warning when the conditions were prevalent for another smog event.

The committee's final report wouldn't be released until a year later in 1954. Beaver's committee further recommended, "smokeless zones" in which some emissions would be prohibited as well as "smoke control areas" in which there would be a restriction on the domestic burning of bituminous coal. Lastly, it also suggested the establishment of

grants to convert domestic fires to more smokeless fuels. However, despite these recommendations, the government still continued to be sluggish in its response. Several MPs, including Gerald Nabarro, then took it upon themselves to introduce a Private Members Bill of the Clean Air Bill, which would be withdrawn after the government promised to introduce its own legislation, which became the Clean Air Act of 1956.

The act instituted several of Beaver's committee's policies, including the "smokeless zones" which would be known as Smoke Control Areas, which limited the burning of various fuels to only those authorised, which included smokeless fuels. Local authorities were charged with implementing the Smoke Control Areas, much to the appreciation of the LCC. The Clean Air Act of 1968 continued the efforts of the original act, amending and extending it as well as requiring future power plants to be built outside of metropolitan areas. Both acts would later be consolidated under the Clean Air Act of 1993. The acts had a great benefit to the city, and while it would be subject to another smog event in 1962, no other events would rise to the level of the Great Smog.

London's air quality gradually improved over the decades so that by the time The Crown aired, the phenomena would seem unreal to the modern Londoner. Not content to use CGI to reproduce the effects, the programme instead built its sets inside a warehouse that was filled with man-made fog. While the events of those five days were exaggerated for drama, the real effects of the Great Smog were indeed terrible and forced the British government to come to terms with the dangers presented by pollution and a lack of regulations. With recent smog events threatening the likes of cities in China and Iran, the view of London's history offered in The Crown still acts as a lesson for modern audiences all over the world.

LONDON BOOKSHOP DREAMS
Adventures in Buying More Books Than My Luggage Can Carry

By Jonathan Thomas

Books are my favorite souvenir from my travels in England. I love picking up new books about England for my library back home. Each book is a tangible reminder of the trip and where it was purchased. Books are also a very affordable souvenir. Did you know that in Britain, there is no tax on books? That's right - the 20% VAT rate is not charged on books. That means that most new paperback books cost under £10. If you were to visit a used books store, they would be even cheaper. One our recent trip, I was determined to visit some bookstores I had not visited before, visit some old haunts and buy as many books as my trip budget would allow.

Stanfords

Stanfords is the first bookstore I visit on every trip to London. Stanfords is a bookstore that specialices solely in travel - guidebooks, travel writing, maps, etc. My main goal for this visit was to find a very large route planning map of the entire British Isles. My current map on the Anglotopia Office wall is well over ten years old and has seen better days. And while I love this particular map, it now out of print, so I need a new one.

Edward Stanford started the store in 1853 as a map seller, and the store expanded from there. It moved to its current location on Long Acre near Covent Garden in 1901. Its stately building is a joy to look at - let alone go inside. Today, every floor of the Victorian building is packed with maps, travel guides, and inspirational travel writing; with beautiful hand-made globes and detailed atlases, as well as essential travel accessories for every occasion.

The ground floor features best sellers and special offers (and you can often find non-travel related books that are currently popular). There's also a great section dedicated solely to London related books. There's often a special buy one, get one-half off sale on the front tables - something I always take advantage of (last year I bought far too many books about British walks). Their British travel section is top notch, and you can find so many lovely books about travel in the UK that you cannot find back home in the USA. My favorite section is the Ordnance Survey Map wall - they literally have every OS map that is printed and a handy guide on how to find the ones for the places you plan to go. OS maps are a must if you plan to do any walking in the English countryside. You can even get custom maps printed in the store while you wait.

The other floors are a dizzying array of travel books on every subject you can imagine. There's the section on travel writing. There's a section for pretty much every country in the world. If there is somewhere you want to go, Stanfords will have a book and map about it.

I found several books that were on my wishlist and also discovered a few more that I didn't know about - those are always the best treats to find at Stanfords. I also visited the map room.

Yes, it's a room just for buying maps.

My goal was to locate a new British Isles route planning map. I went through all the maps in the display cases and was slightly disappointed at first - I could not find one big enough or detailed enough for what I was looking for. And then I found it on the last display. It's a map from 2013 called the UK Route Planning Map by Map Marketing. It features everything I wanted along with great detail. It will be invaluable for future British trip planning. And it was only £20 - not a bad deal for a rolled map.

I purchased about £100 worth of books. See picture above for the specific titles. I also joined their loyalty program which awards points for your purchases. I earned enough on my first go to get £10 off my next purchase or order. Foolishly, I was so excited with all my finds that I forgot to ask if I could have everything shipped home. This was a mistake. All the books could not fit in my luggage, so some friends were kind enough to ship them home for me. The bigger problem was the map. The hotel we were staying at, Hazlitt's, tried to have it sent home but it would have cost something like £40. A ridiculous price for one £20 map. So, to get home, I had to carry the map with me through airport security and keep it with me on the plane. It

OS Explorer Map

LOVERS' LONDON
TICKET TO RIDE
PRISONERS OF GEOGRAPHY
TIM MARSHALL
LONDON STORIES
A LAND OF TWO HALVES
JOE BENNETT
HOW TO READ LONDON
Chris Rogers
THE RAILWAYS
NATION, NETWORK AND PEOPLE
SIMON BRADLEY
The 500 Hidden Secrets of LONDON
LUSTER
LONDON A LIFE IN MAPS
PETER WHITFIELD

FOYLES
FOYLES

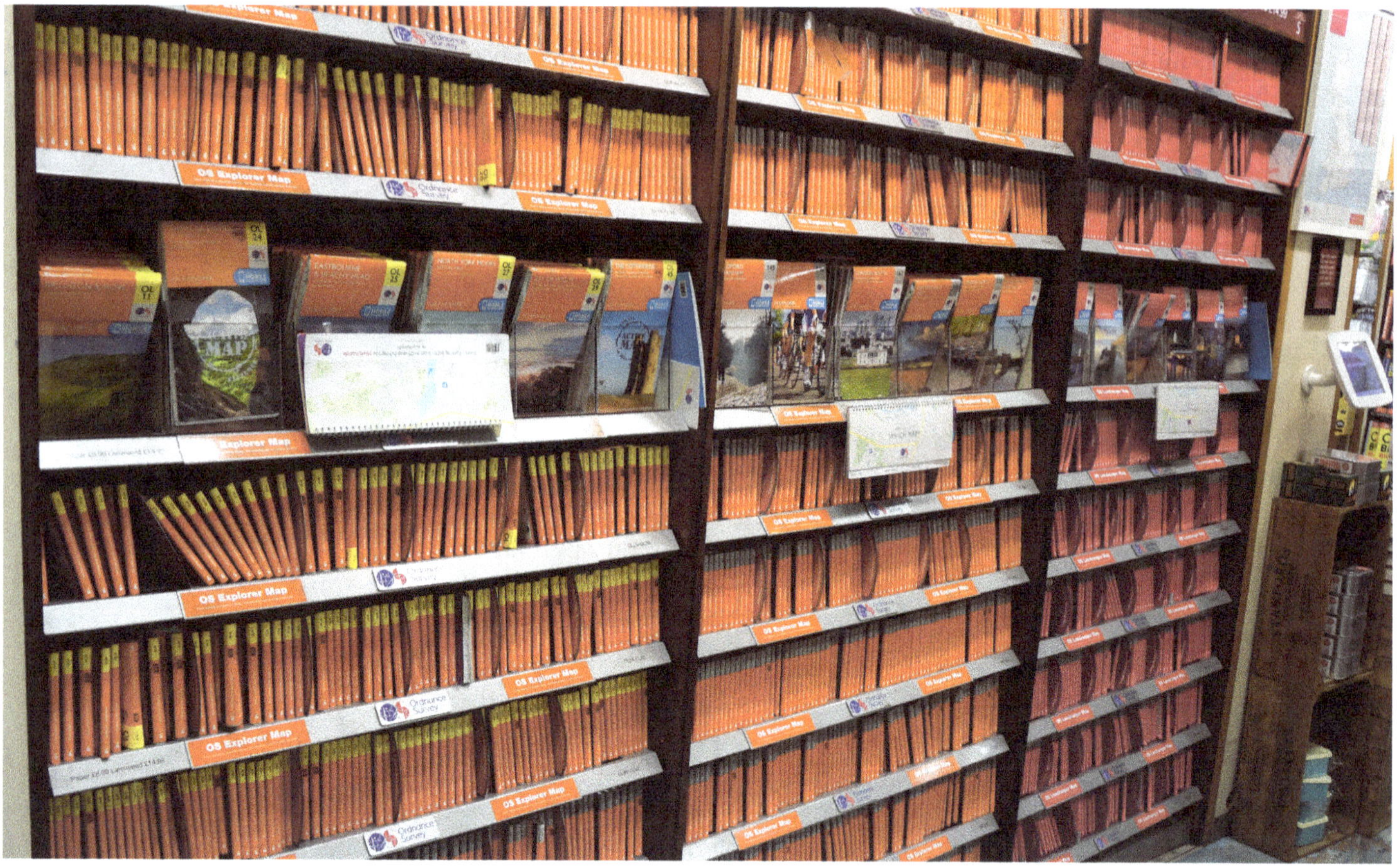

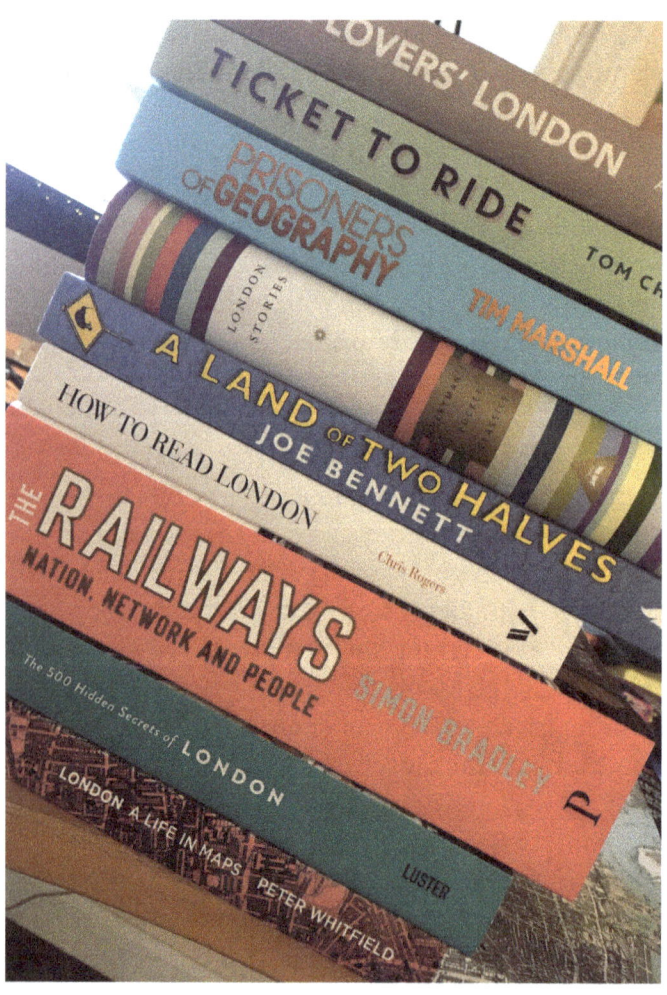

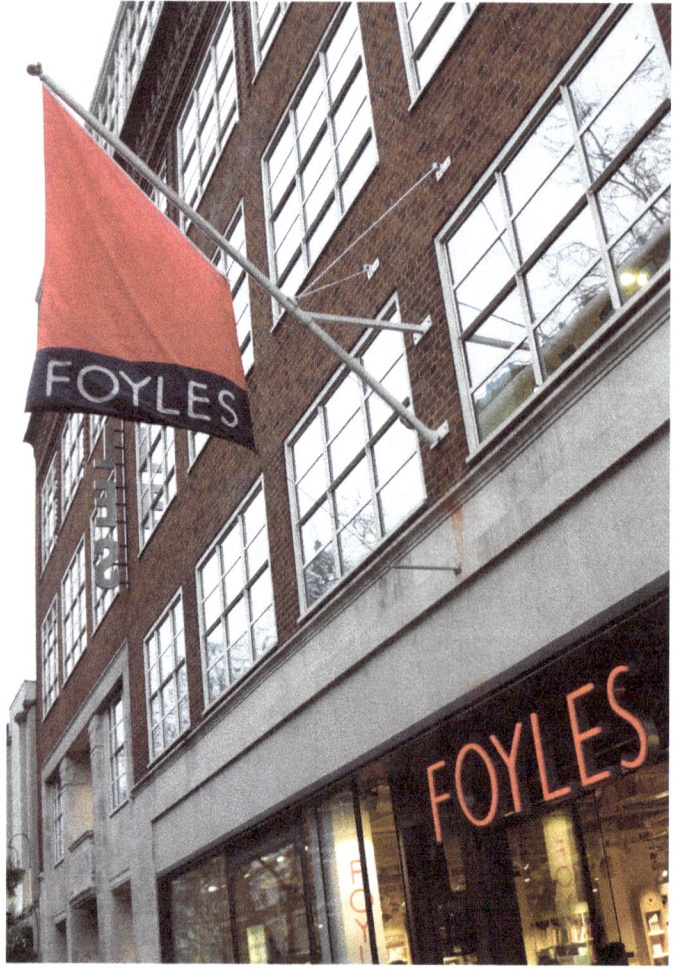

was worth it though; it's a beautiful map.

Foyle's

In 15 years of travel to London, I had never been to Foyle's. I know, as a lover of books this is heresy. They recently moved locations to a bigger store further down Charing Cross Road. I finally decided to make my book pilgrimage to this old icon of London books. I was not disappointed.

Foyle's was founded in 1904 by brothers William and Gilbert Foyle and established them as the literary heart of London. Under Christina Foyle, the store was known for its unique quirks - like forcing you to purchase your books in each department then collect them at a central location. The shop operated a payment system that required customers to get in line three times: to collect an invoice for a book, to pay the invoice, then to collect the book, simply because sales staff were not allowed to handle cash. Equally mystifying to customers was a shelving arrangement that categorised books by publisher, rather than by topic or author. It was said that "if Kafka had been a bookseller, Foyles would have been the result."

When Christina died in 1999, the store began to modernise and act like a traditional bookstore, much to loyal customers relief (despite those who probably enjoyed the quirks). Foyle's has also entered the cultural lexicon of Britain - Foyle's War creator Anthony Horowitz has said that the main character Christopher Foyle is named after the store because the name evoked the 1940s and the archaic practices of the store. Staff, who used to be fired for no reason and turnover was high, now became experts in their fields and service improved at the store. They have since expanded, opening a few outlets around London and the rest of England. The Charing Cross store is still their main headquarters.

When I arrived at Foyle's, it was a rainy Saturday afternoon, so it was the perfect time to get lost in a bookstore. And boy, did I get lost. As their website says, there are more than 200,000 titles in stock in this store. There are six floors of books, divided up by topic area. As someone with particular interests, it was like the store was laid out for me. From the English History section to the travel section to - yes even a special Churchill section. I had no troubles finding books I was looking for and much to my wallet's dismay, finding new books I hadn't heard of.

They also had shopping baskets handy, which helped as my selection of books got larger and larger.

I practically got lost in all the sections related to British history. I was rescued by Mrs. Anglotopia, who found me deciding whether or not to buy certain titles about Churchill. I was particularly impressed with their selection of science fiction. They had a huge selection - not just of current sci-fi hits but also a great selection of back catalog titles. I stocked up on a few titles I had been looking for back home. The kids' section was also amazing, and I picked up a special book for our children.

My only real complaint about the store is that it was very crowded. It was less of a problem as you climbed the staircase and the people started to tail off, but it was hot and stuffy in there. Though it may have just been my excitement. Also, everything is shiny and new. I had heard so many stories about musty old Foyle's; I was surprised to see that the new shop is so modern and clean. Still, it makes it easy to find everything you're looking for.

When it came time to checkout, I could barely carry the basket, so that was my sign to stop and be more sensible. I went to the checkout counter in the history department. This time, I remembered to ask if they could send my books home to the USA. Once again, I'd bought too many to take home in my baggage. They were happy to arrange it - though it cost £40, I bought 20 books in all - so that's not a bad shipping rate. I also joined their 'Foyalty' program, which turns out was a good idea as members got an additional 20% off that weekend, so I saved a ton of money on my, and I'm rather ashamed to admit, large purchase.

Two weeks after my visit, I was still waiting for them to arrive. When I got home, I wrote their customer service email to find out their status - usually, I would be sent a tracking number or confirmation when something was shipped. I received no reply. I tried to contact them on Twitter and also got no reply. I was not very pleased with the customer service at this point. I tried again; this time found the email address for the department where I shipped my books, and I got a quick response that the books had been posted and I should have them any day now. In fact, they arrived that very day, all in the same condition I purchased them.

I liked Foyles very much; I will be back.

Hatchard's

Located practically next door to Fortnum & Mason's, Hatchard's is London oldest bookstore (in fact the UK's oldest) founded in 1797. It has been at its current location since 1801. When you enter for the first time, it's exactly how you imagine an old bookstore in London to be - soft lighting, miles of bookshelves, wood paneling and oil paintings. Hatchard's is famous for its knowledgeable staff. It even has a customised subscription program where they will send you books every month tailored to your tastes. They host many big author-related events throughout the year. Despite its unique character, Hatchard's is not an independent bookstore and hasn't been for many years. It's currently owned by the major bookstore chain Waterstones (and they've opened a second location in St Pancras Station). But this store is not like any other Waterstones, it is and will always be Hatchard's.

I have been to Hatchard's several times and, in fact, I had not planned to visit it on this trip. But as we had a few minutes to kill before seeing a play down the street, we walked by, and I couldn't resist (Mrs. Anglotopia will agree that I have a bookstore problem).

The ground floor is nicely laid out, and I was happy to find their section on British History right near the front. I did not intend to buy too many books because I didn't want to carry them to to the play. But then I got lost in the bookstore and discovered many more books I did not know existed. I climbed through the multiple floors and kept finding more books. Hatchard's is a most dangerous place for booklovers. You only live once,

right?

When I finally went to check out, I had a stack of 10 books, and then their 'impulse' books at the counter roped me in, and I threw in several more. This is me showing restraint. So, now presented with a stack of books too heavy to carry to the theatre, I enquired about sending them home, and they were happy to oblige. I paid, they complimented me on my selection, took my details, and I was off to the theatre. I spent £150 I hadn't planned to when I walked in. Thanks, great exchange rate with the US Dollar, thank you very much.

Of all the books I had sent home, these arrived first. It was one week from when I purchased them to when they showed up at my door. They arrived in a Hatchard's box and were so well bubble-wrapped that all the books arrived in perfect condition. I really appreciated the extra care as airmail can be quite dangerous, even to sturdy books.

Charing Cross Road Second Hand Stores

Charing Cross Road has long been famous as the home of London's bookshops. There was even a fantastic movie about it called 84 Charing Cross Road starring Anthony Hopkins. Time has not been kind to this tradition, and many stores have faded away with time. There's still quite a few lovely specialist bookstores and secondhand stores to be found, however. I popped into a few since my hotel was not far away. My favorite was Quinto & Francis Edwards who had a lovely mix of antiquarian books and second-hand titles. Its floors creaked like you imagine they should, and there's a great old book smell to the place. The staff as friendly. I'll be back!

Also, head down to Cecil Court, which is home to many of London finer booksellers - first editions, signed, and art prints. These are not secondhand stores, and the books you find down this very picturesque street are keepsakes for any library. They're also expensive. It's worth walking down this street just to go for a window shop.

Forbidden Planet & Gosh!

I'm a huge fan of science fiction - books and movies. So, Forbidden Planet is one of my favorite stops in London. The first floor features aisles of the latest movie and TV merchandise for all the major franchises. If you're looking for the latest Doctor Who gear, then this is your place. The bottom floor, however, is book, graphic novel, and comic book heaven. Now, when I'm in London, I try not to buy books that I can easily buy back home. So, exploring a store like Forbidden Planet is more about the spirit of discovery and finding harder to find books. That being said, I managed to find half a dozen sci-fi books that I wanted to take a chance on, several of which I'd never heard of. I was looking for one particular graphic novel - the original Ethel & Earnest by Raymond Briggs (which was the basis of the recent animated film that's fabulous). I could not locate it amongst the thousands of graphic novels they had. So, I asked at the desk, and it turns out it was the one title they did not have. Still, I was not disappointed with my Forbidden Planet haul.

On my way back to my hotel, I wandered the side alleys of Soho in an attempt to learn more about the neighborhood and see what else was around. It was then that I stumbled upon Gosh!, a famous London comic book and graphic novel store that I'd heard of but not yet visited. I popped in to see if they had Ethel & Ernest and sure enough, it was sitting on the main table. I bought that, and only that, showing considerable restraint by not exploring the rest of the very very temptingly cool store. So, that's my adventures book buying in London. I now have enough new books to keep me busy for the next year or so, many new treasures and many new experiences.

WILLIAM MORRIS
The Founder of the Arts & Crafts Movement

Some historic figures, popular during their time, fade into oblivion. Others rise in prestige after their death and influence the future even more than they did their present. William Morris, poet, designer, and activist for a better society, did just that. Mostly known during his time as a poet, those poems are largely forgotten, but his influence on design, architectural preservation, craftsmanship, and the place of the individual in society was profound and made a lasting impression on future generations.

Victorian England was a place of contrasts. The rise of the 'dark satanic mills' of industry swept aside much of the past, and created opportunities for wealth for some, and lives of grinding poverty for many others. But it was also a time of great hope for a better future, and a time populated by idealists, democrats, revolutionaries, and artists. One of the most significant figures on that latter side was born into the former - the son of a wealthy financier who went on to embrace a respect for craftsmanship rooted in a medieval time thought lost and ideals of revolutionary socialism. That figure was William Morris.

Morris was born on 24 March, 1834, into a wealthy middle-class family, and raised mostly at home, a mansion surrounded by gardens and woodlands. From an early age, he read, rode his pony through the woods, and explored the Iron-age remains of a near-mythical British past. His father died when he was 13, and his family moved to a smaller, but still very comfortable house. He was sent to Marlborough College, a newly-opened independent school in Wiltshire, where he missed his mother, was seen as eccentric, and bullied. After a year of misery, he was brought back home and privately tutored there.

He went to study Classics at Exeter College, Oxford, but hated the classes and developed a passion for the medieval period. Britain at this time was in a social crisis. The rise of industrial capitalism, and the consequent destruction of both the physical and social structure of society led many to look for solutions. Morris had a romantic sensibility and was drawn to the idea of the philosopher Thomas Carlyle, who looked to the medieval concepts of chivalry as an antidote to the hard-nosed capitalist ethic. He was also influenced by the ideals of Christian socialism espoused by people such as the author Charles Kingsley.

At Oxford, he met Edward Burne-Jones, whose father was a tradesman. They developed a lifelong friendship. Morris, Burne-Jones, and other students formed a group they called the 'Brotherhood,' now called the Birmingham Set since most of the students came from that city. They met to read Shelley and Keats, recite Shakespeare and Tennyson, and also to read and absorb the aesthetic values of John Ruskin. They travelled to medieval sites across Britain and Europe, often using the financial generosity of Morris for their activities. They toyed with the idea of founding a monastery, but Morris became disillusioned with religious doctrine, and instead, he and Burne-Jones decided on a life committed to art.

Mass-production was a novel idea that grew with the Industrial Revolution, and the market was flooded with cheap, poorly-designed and poorly-made items. Ruskin rejected all this, and instead proposed the elevation of crafts to the level of art, without the standard gradations of art, so that painting and sculpture would not reign supreme. There would be no distinction between a craftsman and an artist, and this ideal appealed to Morris, who saw a romanticised model for it in medieval craftsmanship, where objects of great beauty were made by humble craftsmen.

After graduation, in 1856 Morris joined the offices of architect George Edmund Street, who worked in the new Neo-Gothic style, and studied architectural drawing. Burne-Jones joined the Pre-Raphaelites, an artistic group favoured by John Ruskin, who painted pictures of an idealised medieval world, filled with precise detail. Morris bought many of their paintings. Swept up in a growing progressive movement in the arts, Morris switched from architecture to painting, but his work was not as good as that of his friends, and he began instead to design furniture, illustrate manuscripts and embroider tapestries. He self-published a book of poems, but it sold poorly and was not well-received.

In 1859 he married Jane Burden, a working-class girl who had modelled for him and set about building a house for them. He commissioned a young architect to help him – this was Philip Webb, and the Red House, as it was called, was his first commission. The house was both Neo-Gothic and original, with Webb designing the outside and Morris the interior. It was to become a pivotal

Example of a Morris designed printed textile

design in the movement Morris and his friends created – the Arts & Crafts Movement. The house also took a large chunk out of Morris' personal wealth – about half a million pounds in today's money.

With his friends of similar tastes, he founded Morris, Marshall, Faulkner & Co. in 1861. Calling themselves 'The Firm' they took premises in Red Lion Square, Holborn, and dedicated their business to elevating design to the level of fine art. As part of the broader desire to reform society, the Firm took boys from the 'Industrial Home for Destitute Boys' in nearby Euston and trained them as apprentices. Their work was to be affordable and egalitarian. Neo-Gothic was still battling with the declining Neo-Gothic school, but the Firm won commendations and build numerous stain-glass windows for churches being restored across the country. Besides furniture and murals, Morris was abandoning his painting and moving into wallpaper design – his first design, from 1862, was the famous 'Trellis' pattern still used today.

At home, Morris and Jane had two daughters, who lived an idyllic life in the Red House, but Jane was spending more and more time with the Pre-Raphaelite Dante Gabriel Rossetti, in a relationship that has never been clarified, but which certainly created tensions. The daily commute of several hours from home to London began to wear too, and when the Firm moved to Bloomsbury in 1865, Morris sold the Red House and moved his family into a flat above the Firm's premises. Although they gained some prestigious contracts, the Firm continued to make only a small profit, straining Morris' finances. It was during this time that he met Henry James and Charles Eliot Norton, spreading his ideas to America and creating the American Arts & Crafts Movement. After his early setback, Morris returned to poetry and this time gathered a strong following and good sales with two epic poems, The Life and Death of Jason and The Earthy Paradise. Between 1870 and 1875 he made 18 illuminated manuscripts, entirely by hand in the medieval tradition, developing his calligraphy and raising it to an art-form. By now he had a strong public presence and gave interviews and sat for portraits.

In his private life, it would seem he had accepted his wife's relationship with Rossetti. Indeed, he and Rossetti took a joint-tenancy on a 16th-century country house, Kelmscott Manor, where his wife and children spent much of their time with Rossetti, while Morris visited for short periods. He moved into a London home, Horrington House, in Turnham Green, close to Burne-Jones, who he visited regularly. In 1871, he made the first of several trips to Iceland. He was already deeply involved in Icelandic sagas, having made friends with the Icelandic theologian Eiríkr Magnússon. He and Magnússon visited numerous sites in the country; Morris became a supporter of the Icelandic independence movement and moved more politically towards socialism and ideals of class equality.

Following a final rift with Rossetti, and with other partners moving in their own directions, Morris bought out the partners and re-established the Firm as Morris & Co., under his sole ownership. He also took a renewed interest in architecture and founded the Society for the Protection of Ancient Buildings to encourage preservation, of old buildings, which were being destroyed in the name of Neo-Gothic 'restoration' - which often involved merely adding faux embellishments. This society was to be instrumental in the establishment of the National Trust, whose policies closely mirrored his ideals.

In 1881 he moved his business to Merton Abbey Mills, in the southwest of London. He soon had 100 craftsmen working there, on dying, weaving

His final home at Kelmscott

and making stained glass. Although he had an innovative profit-sharing scheme for senior staff, he was dissatisfied with the level of independent creativity allowed his craftsmen, but felt he was unable to create the socialist workplace he craved, while operating in a capitalist economic system. He was becoming more political and attracted to socialism, which was just beginning to develop in England. He formed the Radical Union, a gathering of several radical working-class groups. He began to lecture on socialism, but when he delivered a speech at Oxford entitled 'Democracy and Art', but which turned into a harangue on socialism, he outraged and shocked the professors and gained national press coverage. He moved towards the radical, revolutionary side of the socialist movement, opposed to the Fabian approach that wanted to peacefully establish socialism through the existing parliamentary system, and formed the Socialist League which advocated an international socialist revolution. Although he began to call himself a communist, by 1890 the League had moved even further left and had been taken over by anarchists, leading Morris to remove his financial support and leave.

Politically distracted, he belatedly recognised that his ideals of craftsmanship were materialising, in the shape of the Art Workers Guild and the spreading of Arts & Crafts as a design-style, and while his firm continued making stained glass, he turned more to writing, creating several novels and founding the Kelmscott Press, dedicated to the production of beautiful books. After several more European trips, his health began to fail, and he withdrew to Kelmscott Manor, where he died of tuberculosis on 4 October, 1896.

His Legacy

Although mourned as a poet after his death, it is as a designer that Morris is chiefly remembered. His influenced in keeping art and design an integral part of modern industrial production cannot be underestimated, and his continuing influence in the promotion of craftsmanship as art still resonates today. His socialist thinking was side-lined by most contemporary admirers of his work, and today it is hardly acknowledged or even remembered by most of those who respect the ideals and output of the Arts & Crafts Movement. His ideas on historic preservation and rural preservation are often cited as precursors of the environmental movement. 20th-century art movements such as Bauhaus owe much to Morris' principles.

Sites to Visit

- Morris' grave is in St George's churchyard in Kelmscott, Oxfordshire.
- The Red House is now a National Trust property on Red House Lane, Bexleyheath, London.
- Kelmscott Manor is open from April to October. It is located in the village of Kelmscott, Gloucestershire.
- There is a Morris Room at the Victoria & Albert Museum in London.

Further Research

- William Morris: Romantic to Revolutionary, by E. P. Thompson and Peter Linebaugh
- Anarchy & Beauty: William Morris and His Legacy, 1860–1960, by Fiona MacCarthy
- William Morris: A Life for Our Time, by Fiona MacCarthy
- William Morris: Poet, Craftsman, Socialist, by Elizabeth Luther Cary

DOWN STREET TUBE STATION
Churchill's Secret Wartime Bunker
By Jonathan Thomas

London's abandoned Tube stations have a special aura about them. It's hard to believe that in a city of eight million people, some tube stations were not used enough to justify staying open. But just because a stationed is abandoned, doesn't mean it can't serve a purpose. And when war is a certainty, every available underground space all of a sudden becomes important. Churchill's Cabinet War Rooms are very much well known, and you can visit them to this day, but what many don't know is that until they were ready for his use, he had another secret bunker - Down Street Tube Station. We had the chance to explore this dark and dangerous place on an organized tour last February. It was a once in a lifetime opportunity.

As with every Tube station, it was originally built with great optimism. The first lines of the London Underground were privately built and funded, so each station was meant to be a money-making proposition. With great fanfare, Down Street Tube Station opened up in 1907 by the Great Northern, Piccadilly and Brompton Railway. It was latterly served by the Piccadilly line and was situated between Dover Street (now named Green Park) and Hyde Park Corner stations. It was designed by Leslie Green in the beautiful Arts & Crafts style of other Piccadilly Line stations. It was thought that a station located just off Pall Mall would be popular with the wealthy residents and guests at the world class hotels located nearby.

What they didn't figure was that wealthy people had no desire to ride the Tube. They had their own means to get around London. The station entrance was also poorly placed because the only place they could fit a station entrance was on Down St, a few hundred feet from Pall Mall itself. Dover St and Hyde Park Corner Stations were not too far away anyway, so people just used those instead. It was simply too inconveniently located to be useful to anyone. As a consequence, the station was little used and was closed in 1932.

Then the war came.

It started to look like war was a distinct possibility in 1938 and preparations began to shore up Britain's infrastructure to ensure continued operations during any kind of attack. Britain's Railways were it's most important national asset so it was decided that the Railway Executive Committee (REC) would be formed to get the railways on a war footing. At this stage in Britain's rail history, this was pre-nationalisation, so all the different rail lines were privately owned and privately competing; they weren't exactly keen to work together. So, it was up to the REC to coordinate amongst the various organizations to ensure continued operations.

The REC needed a secured telephone exchange to allow it to communicate quickly with the various railway companies. It needed bomb proofing and they need space for the Comittee to meet and work 24 hours a day. The plan was to put this new exchange in the basement of their original Westminster headquarters, but this was deemed unsafe due to a flooding risk and the fact the building could not withstand a 500-pound bomb blast. They thought about putting it somewhere in London's suburbs, but they really needed to be as close to the government as possible. Someone had the bright idea that there was a perfectly good Tube station, unused and close to London's poshest hotels and restaurants.

It did not take much to convince the patrician REC Committee Member that this was the ideal solution. A large sum of money was spent to convert the entire below ground station into their new wartime headquarters. The telephone exchange was installed. The elevator shaft and tunnels were reinforced, and living accommodations were installed. The place was to be manned 24 hours, seven days a week. Due to its sensitive nature, employees were required to live on site during their shifts so that the comings and goings wouldn't be obvious to would-be spies. It didn't even have it's own postal address. Dispatches had to be sent via a crack team of motorcyclists always on call, some of whom were women.

The place served it's purpose well, and Britain's railways were able to continue operating during the war, some would say better than before the war! The entire place was a self-contained community with all the provisions they would need (outside of the ration system, I should add). There was a staff canteen which was known to have good food and there was kitchen staff on duty at all hours.

During the London Blitz, which lasted from September 1940 to March 1941, no part of London was safe from German bombs. That included Downing St, the official residence of the Prime Minister which was heavily damaged during the bombing raids. His bunker at the Cabinet War Rooms was not ready. The most important man in

Britain needed somewhere to sleep. The brother of the REC Chair, Sir Ralph Wedgwood convinced Churchill that he would be the safest in the REC's emergency headquarters at Down St.

Churchill spent a total of forty nights during the Blitz in Down Street, taking over the office of one of the committee members as sleeping quarters. The railway hotels serviced the facility, so the food and drink were up to Churchill's standard, and it was said that he rather liked the accommodations, he always made the best of any situation as best he could. He liked the place so much that he arranged to have new personal quarters built for his future use. Alas, they went unused as once the Cabinet War Rooms were completed, he did not need to visit Down St again.

After the war, the REC no longer needed the facility, and it was returned to the London Underground which used it as an engineering access area for the Piccadilly Line. Most of the fittings and fixtures from the war were removed, but elements remain in place, an eerie reminder of Britain's wartime past. The most amazing treasure down there are the remains of the telephone exchange, a beautiful piece of mechanical 20th-century engineering history. There are other bits and bobs from its human habitations, from bath tubs, boilers and the ruins of the kitchen. It's very bizarre to think of all the people working down here, doing their bit for the war as bombs well down from above.

We went down in a tour group of ten people, from all over Britain - and even one fellow who flew in from the Netherlands - so it was an intimate tour. Our tour guide has done the tour almost 100 times, so he's old hat. The station is not suitable for 'tourist' consumption. It's dark, dirty, and dangerous. If a Tube train passed, we had to turn out our flashlights, which made it even darker. It was dusty, loud and beautiful. The station is occasionally open for tours through Hidden London, part of the London Transport Museum. The tickets often sell out a year or so in advance, but you can keep an eye on their website to find out when tickets will be available again. If you have any interest in London's transport and wartime history, I cannot recommend doing this tour more highly.

Photos: From Top To Bottom - 1. The stairs down to the platforms. 2. Directions to wayward employees 3. The former committe room, notice the concrete outlines of the room on the floor. 4. More stairs to the platforms. Opposite page: Old exit sign.

The vintage telephone exchange, left just as it was at the end of the war.

The street level entrance, now a mini-mart with flats above.

The tiles are wearing away with time and grime thanks to the constantly passing Tube trains.

They had to build concrete platforms to make use of the spaces properly.

THE SLANG PAGE
British Sporting Terms and Leagues

The British sporting world is diverse - the Brits, after all, invented many sports the world loves to play. Here is a guide to some common words and phrases you'll encounter.

Association Football - The official name for football or soccer as it is called in the USA.

FA - The official governing body of football; they set the rules and run the leagues.

English Premier League - The Premier League is an English professional league for men's association football clubs. At the top of the English football league system, it is the country's primary football competition. Contested by 20 clubs with a system of relegation for underperforming clubs.

ECB - England Cricket Board - The governing body of Cricket in England and Wales.

The Ashes - The Ashes is a Test cricket series played between England and Australia that is very widely watched. The Ashes are regarded as being held by the team that most recently won the Test series. Held every four years, next will be in 2017-18.

Test Cricket - Test cricket is the longest form of the sport of cricket and is considered its highest standard. Test matches are played between national teams with "Test status," as determined by the International Cricket Council (ICC). The 2 teams of 11 players play a 4-innings match, which may last up to 5 days. The name Test stems from the long, grueling match being a "test" of the relative strengths of the two sides.

Six Nations - The Six Nations Championship is an annual international rugby union competition involving six European sides: England, France, Ireland, Italy, Scotland, and Wales.

Rugby Union - Rugby union, is a contact team sport which originated in England in the first half of the 19th century. One of the two codes of rugby football, it is based on running with the ball in hand. In its most common form, a game is between two teams of 15 players using an oval-shaped ball on a rectangular field with H-shaped goalposts on each try line.

Rugby League - Rugby league football is a full contact sport played by two teams of 13 players on a rectangular field. One of the two codes of rugby football, it originated in England in 1895 as a split from the Rugby Football Union over the issue of payments to players. Its rules gradually changed with the aim of producing a faster, more entertaining game for spectators. In rugby league, points are scored by carrying the ball and touching it to the ground beyond the opposing team's goal line; this is called a try and is the primary method of scoring

FIFA - The official international body that manages the rules and regulations of Football. They also set up the framework for each country's national team.

UEFA - The Union of European Football Associations is the administrative body for association football in Europe, although several member states are primarily or entirely located in Asia. It is one of six continental confederations of world football's governing body FIFA. UEFA consists of 55 national association members.

World Cup - International Competition held every four years where the top national teams compete for the world championship. Run by FIFA. Next will be in 2018.

UEFA European Championship (Euro Cup) - Championship competition featuring national teams from European countries only, held every four years and managed by UEFA. Usually held two years after/before the next World Cup. Next will begin 2020.

Rugby World Cup - The Rugby World Cup is a men's rugby union tournament contested every four years between the top international teams. The tournament was first held in 1987 when the tournament was co-hosted by New Zealand and Australia. New Zealand is the current champion, having defeated Australia in the final of the 2015 tournament.

Wimbledon - General term for The Championships, Wimbledon, the oldest tennis tournament held in the world every June.

All England Club - The All England Lawn Tennis and Croquet Club, also known as the All-England Club, based at Church Road, Wimbledon, London, England, is a private members' club. It is best known as the venue for the Wimbledon Championships, the only Grand Slam tennis event still held on grass.

Snooker - Snooker is a cue sport which originated in India in the 19th century. It is played on a table covered with a green cloth, or baize, with pockets at each of the four corners and in the middle of each side cushion. Using a cue and 22 colored balls, players must strike the white ball to pot the remaining balls in the correct sequence, accumulating points for each pot.

The Boat Race - The Boat Race is an annual rowing race between the Oxford University Boat Club and the Cambridge University Boat Club, rowed between men's open-weight eights on the River Thames in London, England. It is also known as the University Boat Race and the Oxford and Cambridge Boat Race.

www.ingramcontent.com/pod-product-compliance
Lightning Source LLC
Chambersburg PA
CBHW050629120526
44589CB00037BC/2717